The Wild Gallant by John Dryden

John Dryden was born on August 9th, 1631 in the village rectory of Aldwincle near Thrapston in Northamptonshire. As a boy Dryden lived in the nearby village of Titchmarsh, Northamptonshire. In 1644 he was sent to Westminster School as a King's Scholar.

Dryden obtained his BA in 1654, graduating top of the list for Trinity College, Cambridge that year.

Returning to London during The Protectorate, Dryden now obtained work with Cromwell's Secretary of State, John Thurloe.

At Cromwell's funeral on 23 November 1658 Dryden was in the company of the Puritan poets John Milton and Andrew Marvell. The setting was to be a sea change in English history. From Republic to Monarchy and from one set of lauded poets to what would soon become the Age of Dryden.

The start began later that year when Dryden published the first of his great poems, Heroic Stanzas (1658), a eulogy on Cromwell's death.

With the Restoration of the Monarchy in 1660 Dryden celebrated in verse with Astraea Redux, an authentic royalist panegyric.

With the re-opening of the theatres after the Puritan ban, Dryden began to also write plays. His first play, The Wild Gallant, appeared in 1663 but was not successful. From 1668 on he was contracted to produce three plays a year for the King's Company, in which he became a shareholder. During the 1660s and '70s, theatrical writing was his main source of income.

In 1667, he published Annus Mirabilis, a lengthy historical poem which described the English defeat of the Dutch naval fleet and the Great Fire of London in 1666. It established him as the pre-eminent poet of his generation, and was crucial in his attaining the posts of Poet Laureate (1668) and then historiographer royal (1670).

This was truly the Age of Dryden, he was the foremost English Literary figure in Poetry, Plays, translations and other forms.

In 1694 he began work on what would be his most ambitious and defining work as translator, The Works of Virgil (1697), which was published by subscription. It was a national event.

John Dryden died on May 12th, 1700, and was initially buried in St. Anne's cemetery in Soho, before being exhumed and reburied in Westminster Abbey ten days later.

Index of Contents

EDITOR'S PREFACE

The Editor may be pardoned in bestowing remarks upon Dryden's plays, only in proportion to their intrinsic merit, and to the attention which each has excited, either at its first appearance, or when the public attention has been since directed towards them. In either point of view, little need be said on the "Wild Gallant." It was Dryden's first theatrical production, and its reception by no means augured his future pre-eminence in literature; nor was it more than tolerated, when afterwards revived under the sanction of his increasing fame. It was brought upon the stage in February 1662-3, according to the conjecture of Mr Malone, who observes, that the following lines in the prologue.

It should have been but one continued song;
Or, at the least, a dance of three hours long;

must refer to D'Avenant's opera, called the "Siege of Rhodes," acted in 1662; and that the expression, "in plays, he finds, you love mistakes," alludes to the blunders of Teague, an Irish footman, in Sir Robert Howard's play of the "Committee." The "Wild Gallant" was revived and published in 1669, with a new prologue and epilogue, and some other alterations, not of a nature, judging from the prologue, to improve the morality of the piece. That the play had but indifferent success in the action, the poet himself has informed us, with the qualifying addition, that it more than once was the divertisement of Charles II., by his own command. This honourable distinction it probably acquired by the influence of the Countess of Castlemaine, then the royal favourite, to whom Dryden addresses some verses on her encouraging this play.--See Vol. XI p. 18.--The plot is borrowed avowedly from the Spanish, and partakes of the unnatural incongruity, common to the dramatic pieces of that nation, as also of the bustle and intrigue, with which they are usually embroiled. Few modern audiences would endure the absurd grossness of the deceit practised on Lord Nonsuch in the fourth act; nor is the plot of Lady Constance, to gain her lover, by marrying him in the disguise of a heathen divinity, more grotesque than unnatural.--Yet, in the under characters, some liveliness of dialogue is maintained; and the reader may be amused with particular scenes, though, as a whole, the early fate of the play was justly merited. These passages, in which the plot stands still, while the spectators are entertained with flippant dialogue and repartee, are ridiculed in the scene betwixt Prince Prettyman and Tom Thimble in the Rehearsal; the facetious Mr Bibber being the original of the latter personage. The character of Trice, at least his whimsical humour of drinking, playing at dice by himself, and quarrelling as if engaged with a successful gamester, is imitated from the character of Carlo, in Jonson's "Every Man out of his Humour," who drinks with a supposed companion, quarrels about the pledge, and tosses about the cups and flasks in the imaginary brawl. We have heard similar frolics related of a bon-vivant of the last generation, inventor of a game called solitaire, who used to complain of the hardship of drinking by himself, because the toast came too often about.

The whole piece seems to have been intended as a sacrifice to popular taste; and, perhaps, our poet only met a deserved fate, when he stooped to sooth the depraved appetite, which his talents enabled him to have corrected and purified. Something like this feeling may be interred from the last lines of the second epilogue:

Would you but change, for serious plot and verse,
This motley garniture of fool and farce;
Nor scorn a mode, because 'tis taught at home,
Which dues, like vests,[A] our gravity become;
Our poet yields you should this play refuse,
As tradesmen by the change of fashions lose,
With some content, their fripperies of France,
In hope it may their staple trade advance.

[Footnote A: This seems to allude to the Polish dress, which, upon his restoration, Charles wished to introduce into Britain. It was not altered for the French, till his intimacy with that court was cemented by pecuniary dependence.]

In the prologue, the author indulges himself in a display of the terms of astrology, of which vain science he was a believer and a student.

Walter Scott, editor.

PREFACE

It would be a great impudence in me to say much of a comedy, which has had but indifferent success in the action. I made the town my judges, and the greater part condemned it: after which, I do not think it my concernment to defend it with the ordinary zeal of a poet for his decried poem. Though Corneille is more resolute in his preface before his Pertharite[A], which was condemned more universally than this; for he avows boldly, that, in spite of censure, his play was well and regularly written; which is more than I dare say for mine. Yet it was received at court; and was more than once the divertisement of his Majesty, by his own command; but I have more modesty than to ascribe that to my merit, which was his particular act of grace. It was the first attempt I made in dramatic poetry; and, I find since, a very bold one, to begin with comedy, which is the most difficult part of it. The plot was not originally my own; but so altered by me, (whether for the better or worse I know not) that whoever the author was, he could not have challenged a scene of it. I doubt not but you will see in it the uncorrectness of a young writer; which is yet but a small excuse for him, who is so little amended since. The best apology I can make for it, and the truest, is only this, that you have, since that time, received with applause, as bad, and as uncorrect plays from other men.

[Footnote A: "Le succés de cette tragédie à été si malheureux, que pour m'epargner le chagrin de m'en souvenir, je n'en dirai presque rien.--J'ajoute ici malgré sa disgrace, que les sentimens en sont assez vifs et nobles, les vers assez bien tournes, et que la façon dont le sujet s'explique dans la première scène ne manque pas d'artifice."

Examen de Pertharite.]

PROLOGUE, WHEN IT WAS FIRST ACTED

Is it not strange to hear a poet say,
He comes to ask you, how you like the play?
You have not seen it yet: alas! 'tis true;
But now your love and hatred judge, not you:
And cruel factions (bribed by interest) come,
Not to weigh merit, but to give their doom.
Our poet, therefore, jealous of th' event,
And (though much boldness takes) not confident,
Has sent me, whither you, fair ladies, too,
Sometimes upon as small occasions, go;
And, from this scheme, drawn for the hour and day,
Bid me enquire the fortune of his play.

The curtain drawn discovers two Astrologers; the prologue is presented to them.

1st ASTROLOGER – [Reads] A figure of the heavenly bodies in their several Apartments, Feb. the 5th, half-an-hour after three afternoon, from whence you are to judge the success of a new play, called the Wild Gallant.

2nd ASTROLOGER - Who must judge of it, we, or these gentlemen?
We'll not meddle with it, so tell your poet.
Here are, in this house, the ablest mathematicians in Europe for his purpose.
They will resolve the question, ere they part.

1st ASTROLOGER – Yet let us judge it by the rules of art;
First Jupiter, the ascendant's lord disgraced,
In the twelfth house, and near grim Saturn placed,
Denote short life unto the play:--

2nd ASTROLOGER - Jove yet,
In his apartment Sagittary, set
Under his own root, cannot take much wrong.

1st ASTROLOGER - Why then the life's not very short, nor long;

2nd ASTROLOGER - The luck not very good, nor very ill;

PROLOGUE - That is to say, 'tis as 'tis taken still.

1st ASTROLOGER – But, brother, Ptolemy the learned says,
'Tis the fifth house from whence we judge of plays.
Venus, the lady of that house, I find
Is Peregrine; your play is ill-designed;
It should have been but one continued song,
Or, at the least, a dance of three hours long.

2nd ASTROLOGER - But yet the greatest mischief does remain,
The twelfth apartment bears the lords of Spain;
Whence I conclude, it is your author's lot,
To be endangered by a Spanish plot.

PROLOGUE - Our poet yet protection hopes from you,
But bribes you not with any thing that's new;
Nature is old, which poets imitate,
And, for wit, those, that boast their own estate,
Forget Fletcher and Ben before them went,
Their elder brothers, and that vastly spent;
So much, 'twill hardly be repair'd again,
Not, though supplied with all the wealth of Spain,
This play is English, and the growth your own;
As such, it yields to English plays alone.
He could have wish'd it better for your sakes,
But that, in plays, he finds you love mistakes:
Besides, he thought it was in vain to mend,
What you are bound in honour to defend;
That English wit, howe'er despised by some,
Like English valour, still may overcome.

PROLOGUE, WHEN REVIVED

As some raw squire, by tender mother bred,
'Till one-and-twenty keeps his maidenhead;
(Pleased with some sport, which he alone does find;
And thinks a secret to all humankind;)
'Till mightily in love, yet half afraid,
He first attempts the gentle dairy maid:
Succeeding there, and, led by the renown
Of Whetston's park, he comes at length to town;
Where entered, by some school-fellow or friend,
He grows to break glass windows in the end:
His valour too, which with the watch began,
Proceeds to duel, and he kills his man.
By such degrees, while knowledge he did want,
Our unfledged author writ a Wild Gallant.
He thought him monstrous lewd, (I lay my life)
Because suspected with his landlord's wife;

But, since his knowledge of the town began,
He thinks him now a very civil man;
And, much ashamed of what he was before,
Has fairly play'd him at three wenches more.
'Tis some amends his frailties to confess;
Pray pardon him his want of wickedness:
He's towardly, and will come on apace;
His frank confession shows he has some grace.
You baulked him when he was a young beginner,
And almost spoiled a very hopeful sinner;
But if once more you slight his weak endeavour,
For aught I know, he may turn tail forever;

DRAMATIS PERSONAE

Lord NONSUCH, an old rich humorous lord.
Justice TRICE, his neighbour.
Mr LOVEBY, the Wild Gallant.
Sir TIMOROUS, a bashful knight.
FAILER, } hangers-on of Sir TIMOROUS.
BURR,   }
BIBBER, a tailor.
SETSTONE, a jeweller.
Lady CONSTANCE, Lord NONSUCH'S daughter,
Madam ISABELLA, her cousin.
Mrs BIBBER, the tailors wife.
Serjeants, Boy to LOVEBY, Servants, a Bawd and
Whores, Watch and Constable.

SCENE - London

ACT I

SCENE I

FAILER entering to BURR, who is putting on his buff-coat.

FAILER - What! not ready yet, man?

BURR - You do not consider my voyage from Holland last night.

FAILER - Pish, a mere ferry; get up, get up: My cousin's maids will come and blanket thee anon; art thou not ashamed to lie a-bed so long?

BURR - I may be more ashamed to rise; and so you'll say, dear heart, if you look upon my clothes: the best is, my buff-coat will cover all.

FAILER - Egad, there goes more cunning than one would think to the putting thy clothes together. Thy doublet and breeches are Guelphs and Ghibellins to one another; and the stitches of thy doublet are so far asunder, that it seems to hang together by the teeth. No man could ever guess to what part of the body these fragments did belong, unless he had been acquainted with 'em as long as thou hast been. If they once lose their hold, they can never get together again, except by chance the rags hit the tallies of one another. He, that gets into thy doublet, must not think to do it by storm; no, he must win it inch by inch, as the Turk did Rhodes.

BURR - You are very merry with my wardrobe; but, till I am provided of a better, I am resolved to receive all visits in this truckle-bed.

FAILER - Then will I first scotch the wheels of it, that it may not run: Thou hast cattle enough in it to carry it down stairs, and break thy neck; 'tis got a yard nearer the door already.

Enter Boy.

BOY - Sir, Mr Bibber your tailor's below, and desires to speak with you.

FAILER - He's an honest fellow, and a fashionable; he shall set thee forth, I warrant thee.

BURR - Ay; but where's the money for this, dear heart?

FAILER - Well, but what think you of being put into a suit of clothes without money? [Aside.

BURR - You speak of miracles.

FAILER - Do you not know Will Bibber's humour?

BURR - Pr'ythee, what have I to do with his humour?

FAILER - Break but a jest, and he'll beg to trust thee for a suit; nay, he will contribute to his own destruction, and give thee occasions to make one. He has been my artificer these three years; and, all the while, I have lived upon his favourable apprehension. Boy, conduct him up. [Exit Boy.

BURR - But what am I the better for this? I ne'er made jest in all my life.

FAILER - A bare clinch will serve the turn; a car-wichet, a quarter-quibble, or a pun.

BURR - Wit from a Low Country soldier! One, that has conversed with none but dull Dutchmen these ten years! What an unreasonable rogue art thou? why, I tell thee, 'tis as difficult to me, as to pay him ready money.

FAILER - Come, you shall be ruled for your own good; I'll throw the clothes over you to help meditation. And, upon the first opportunity, start you up, and surprise him with a jest.

BURR - Well, I think this impossible to be done: but, however, I'll attempt. [Lies down, FAILER covers him.

FAILER - Husht! he's coming up.

Enter BIBBER.

BIBBER - 'Morrow, Mr Failer: What, I warrant you think I come a dunning now?

FAILER - No, I vow to gad, Will; I have a better opinion of thy wit, than to think thou would'st come to so little purpose.

BIBBER - Pretty well that: No, no, my business is to drink my morning's-draught in sack with you.

FAILER - Will not ale serve thy turn, Will?

BIBBER - I had too much of that last night; I was a little disguised, as they say.

FAILER - Why disguised? Hadst thou put on a clean band, or washed thy face lately? Those are thy disguises, Bibber.

BIBBER - Well, in short, I was drunk; damnably drunk with ale; great hogan-mogan bloody ale: I was porterly drunk, and that I hate of all things in nature.

Burr, rising.] And of all things in nature I love it best.

BIBBER - Art thou there, i'faith? and why, old boy?

BURR - Because, when I am porterly drunk, I can carry myself.

BIBBER - Ha, ha, boy.

FAILER - This porter brings sad news to you, Will; you must trust him for a suit of clothes, as bad as 'tis: Come, he's an honest fellow, and loves the king.

BIBBER - Why, it shall be my suit to him, that I may trust him.

BURR - I grant your suit, sir.

FAILER - Burr, make haste and dress you; Sir Timorous dines here to-day: you know him?

BURR - Aye, aye, a good honest young fellow; but no conjurer; he and I are very kind.

FAILER - Egad, we two have a constant revenue out of him: He would now be admitted suitor to my Lady Constance Nonsuch, my Lord Nonsuch's daughter; our neighbour here in Fleetstreet.

BURR - Is the match in any forwardness?

FAILER - He never saw her before yesterday, and will not be brought to speak to her this month yet.

BURR - That's strange.

FAILER - Such a bashful knight did I never see; but we must move for him.

BIBBER - They say, here's a great dinner to be made to-day here, at your cousin Trice's, on purpose for the interview.

BURR - What, he keeps up his old humour still?

FAILER - Yes, certain; he admires eating and drinking well, as much as ever, and measures every man's wit by the goodness of his palate.

BURR - Who dines here besides?

FAILER - Jack Loveby.

BIBBER - O, my guest.

BURR - He has ever had the repute of a brave clear-spirited fellow.

FAILER - He's one of your Dear Hearts, a debauchee.

BURR - I love him the better for't: The best heraldry of a gentleman is a clap, derived to him from three generations. What fortune has he?

FAILER - Good fortune at all games; but no estate: He had one; but he has made a devil on't long ago. He's a bold fellow, I vow to gad: A person, that keeps company with his betters; and commonly has gold in's pockets. Come, Bibber, I see thou longest to be at thy morning's watering: I'll try what credit I have with the butler.

BIBBER - Come away, my noble Festus and new customer.

FAILER - Now will he drink, till his face be no bigger than a three-pence.

[Exeunt.

SCENE II

Enter LOVEBY and BOY; followed by FRANCES, BIBBER'S wife.

LOVEBY - Nay, the devil take thee, sweet landlady, hold thy tongue: Was't not enough thou hast scolded me from my lodging, which, as long as I rent it, is my castle; but to follow me here to Mr Trice's, where I am invited; and to discredit me before strangers, for a lousy, paltry sum of money?

FRANCES - I tell you truly, Mr Loveby, my husband and I cannot live by love, as they say; we must have wherewithal, as they say; and pay for what we take; or some shall smoke fort.

LOVEBY - Smoke! why a piece of hung beef in Holland is not more smoked, than thou hast smoked me already. Thou knowest I am now fasting; let me have but fair play; when I have lined my sides with a good dinner, I'll engage upon reputation to come home again, and thou shall scold at me all the afternoon.

FRANCES - I'll take the law on you.

LOVEBY - The law allows none to scold in their own causes: What dost thou think the lawyers take our money for?

FRANCES - I hope you intend to deal by my husband like a gentleman, as they say?

LOVEBY - Then I should beat him most unmercifully, and not pay him neither.

FRANCES - Come, you think to fobb me off with your jests, as you do my husband; but it won't be: yonder he comes, and company with him. Husband, husband! why, William, I say!

Enter BIBBER, BURR, and FAILER, at the other end.

LOVEBY - Speak softly, and I will satisfy thee.

FRANCES - You shall not satisfy me, sir; pay me for what you owe me, for chamber-rent and diet, and many a good thing besides, that shall be nameless.

LOVEBY - What a stygian woman's this, to talk thus? Hold thy tongue 'till they be gone, or I'll cuckold thy husband.

FRANCES - You cuckold him--would you durst cuckold him! I will not hold my tongue, sir.

BIBBER - Yonder's my guest; what say you, gentlemen? Shall I call him to go down with us?

LOVEBY - I must make a loose from her, there's no other way. Save ye, Mr Failer; is your cousin Trice stirring yet? Answer me quickly, sir, is your cousin Trice yet stirring?

FAILER - I'll go and see, sir. Sure the man has a mind to beat me; but I vow to gad I have no mind to be beaten by him. Come away, Burr. Will, you follow us.

BIBBER - I'll be with you immediately.

[Exeunt BURR and FAILER.

LOVEBY - Who was that with Failer, Will?

BIBBER - A man at arms, that's come from Holland.

LOVEBY - A man out at arms thou mean'st, Will.

BIBBER - Good, i'faith.

FRANCES - Aye, aye; you run questing up and down after your gambols, and your jests, William; and never mind the main chance, as they say: Pray get in your debts, and think upon your wife and children.

LOVEBY - Think upon the sack at Carey-house, with the Abricot flavour, Will. Hang a wife; what is she, but a lawful kind of manslayer? Every little hug in bed is a degree of murdering thee: and for thy children, fear 'em not: thy part of 'em shall be taylors, and they shall trust; and those, thy customers get for thee, shall be gentlemen, and they shall be trusted by their brethren; and so thy children shall live by one another.

BIBBER - Did you mark that, Frances? There was wit now; he call'd me cuckold to my face, and yet for my heart I cannot be angry with him. I perceive you love Frances, sir; and I love her the better for your sake; speak truly, do you not like such a pretty brown kind of woman?

LOVEBY - I do i'faith, Will; your fair women have no substance in 'em, they shrink in the wetting.

FRANCES - Well, you may be undone if you will, husband: I hear there are two or three actions already out against him: You may be the last, if you think good.

BIBBER - Tis true she tells me; I love your wit well, sir; but I must cut my coat according to my cloth.

FRANCES - Sir, we'll come by our own as we can; if you put us oft' from week to week thus.

LOVEBY - Nay, but good landlady--

FRANCES - Will good landlady set on the pot, as they say; or make the jack go? then I'll hear you.

BIBBER - Now she's too much on t'other hand; hold your prating, Frances; or I'll put you out of your Pater Nosters, with a sorrow to you.

FRANCES - I did but lay the law open to him, as they say, whereby to get our money in: But if you knew how he had used me, husband!

BIBBER - Has he used you, Frances? put so much more into his bill for lodging.

LOVEBY - Honest Will, and so he died[A]; I thank thee, little Bibber, being sober, and, when I am drunk, I will kiss thee for't. [Footnote A: This expression seems proverbial.]

BIBBER - Thank me, and pay me my money, sir; though I could not forbear my jest, I do not intend to lose by you; if you pay me not the sooner, I must provide you another lodging; say I give you warning.

LOVEBY - Against next quarter, landlord?

BIBBER - Of an hour, sir.

LOVEBY - That's short warning, Will.

BIBBER - By this hand you shall up into the garret, where the little bed is; I'll let my best room to a better pay-master: you know the garret, sir?

FRANCES - Aye, he knows it, by a good token, husband.

LOVEBY - I sweat to think of that garret, Will; thou art not so unconscionable to put me there? Why, 'tis a kind of little ease[B], to cramp thy rebellious prentices in; I have seen an usurer's iron chest would hold two on't: A penny looking-glass cannot stand upright in the window, that and the brush tills it: the hat-case must be disposed under the bed, and the comb-case will hang down, from the ceiling to the floor. If I chance to dine in my chamber, I must stay till I am empty before I can get out: and if I chance to spill the chamber-pot, it will overflow it from top to bottom. [Footnote B: A kind of dungeon, so called from its construction.]

BIBBER - Well, for the description of the garret, I'll bate you something of the bill.

LOVEBY - All, all, good Will; or, to stay thy fury till my rents come up, I will describe thy little face.

BIBBER - No, rather describe your own little money; I am sure that's so little it is not visible.

LOVEBY - You are in the right, I have not a cross at present, as I am a sinner; an you will not believe me, I'll turn my pockets inside outward--Ha! What's the meaning of this? my pockets heavy! has my small officer put in counters to abuse me?--How now! yellow boys, by this good light? sirrah, varlet, how came I by this gold? Ha!

BOY - What gold do you mean, sir? the devil a piece you had this morning. In these last three weeks, I have almost forgot what my teeth were made for; last night good Mrs Bibber here took pity on me, and crumm'd me a mess of gruel with the children, and I popt and popt my spoon three or four times to my mouth, before I could find the way to't.

LOVEBY - 'Tis strange, how I should come by so much money! [Aside.] Has there been nobody about my chamber this morning, landlady?

BOY - O yes, sir; I forgot to tell you that: This morning a strange fellow, as ever eyes beheld, would needs come up to you, when you were asleep; but when he came down again, he said, he had not waked you.

LOVEBY - Sure this fellow, whoe'er he was, was sent by Fortune to mistake me into so much money. Well, this is not the first time my necessities have been strangely supplied: some Cadua or other has a kindness for me, that's certain: [Aside.]--Well, Mons. Bibber, from henceforward I'll keep my wit for more refined spirits; you shall be paid with dirt;--there's money for you.

BIBBER - Nay, good sir.

LOVEBY - What's your sum? tell it out: will the money burn your fingers? Sirrah, boy, fetch my suit with the gold-lace at sleeves, from tribulation.

[Gives him gold. Exit BOY.] Mr Taylor, I shall turn the better bill-man[A], and knock that little coxcomb of yours, if you do not answer me what I owe you. [Footnote A: Alluding to the ancient weapon called the bill; a never-failing source of puns in old plays.]

BIBBER - Pray, sir, trouble not yourself; 'tis nothing; i'feck now 'tis not.

LOVEBY - How nothing, sir?

FRANCES - An't, please your worship, it was seventeen pounds and a noble yesterday at noon, your worship knows: And then your worship came home ill last night, and complained of your worship's head; and I sent for three dishes of tea for your good worship, and that was six pence more, and please your worship's honour.

LOVEBY - Well; there's eighteen pieces, tell 'em.

BIBBER - I say, Frances, do not take 'em.

LOVEBY - What, is all your pleading of necessity come to this?

BIBBER - Now I see he will pay, he shall not pay. Frances, go home, and fetch him the whole bag of forty pounds; I'll lend it him, and the lease of the house too; he shall want for nothing.

LOVEBY - Take the money, or I'll leave your house.

BIBBER - Nay, rather than displease his worship, take it. [She takes it.

LOVEBY - So, so; go home quietly and suckle my godson, Frances. [Exit FRANCES.

BIBBER - If you are for the cellar, sir, you know the way. [Exit BIBBER.

LOVEBY - No, my first visit shall be to my mistress, the Lady Constance Nonsuch. She's discreet, and how the devil she comes to love me, I know not; yet I am pretty confident she loves me. Well, no woman can be wiser, than you-know-what will give her leave to be.

Enter Lady CONSTANCE, and Madam ISABELLA.

ISABELLA - Look, look; is not that your servant Loveby?

LOVEBY - Tis she; there's no being seen, 'till I am better habited. [Exit LOVEBY.

CONSTANCE - Let him go, and take no notice of him: Poor rogue! he little thinks I know his poverty.

ISABELLA - And less, that you supply it by an unknown hand.

CONSTANCE - Aye, and falsified my father's key to do it.

ISABELLA - How can you answer this to your discretion?

CONSTANCE - Who could see him want, she loves?

Enter SETSTONE.

ISABELLA - O here's Mr Setstone come, your jeweller, madam.

CONSTANCE - Welcome, Setstone; hast thou performed thy visit happily, and without discovery?

SETSTONE - As you would wish it, madam: I went up to his chamber without interruption; and there found him drowning his cares, and pacifying his hunger, with sleep; which advantage I took, and; undiscovered by him, left the gold divided in his pockets.

CONSTANCE - Well, this money will furnish him, I hope, that we may have his company again.

SETSTONE - Two hundred and fifty good pounds, madam. Has your father missed it yet?

CONSTANCE - No; if he had, we should have all heard on't before now: But, pray God Monsieur Loveby has no other haunts to divert him, now he's ransomed! What a kind of woman is his landlady?

SETSTONE - Well enough to serve a tailor; or to kiss when he comes home drunk, or wants money; but far unlikely to create jealousy in your ladyship.

Enter Servant.

SERVANT - Madam, Justice Trice desires your ladyship's excuse, that he has not yet performed the civilities of his hour to you; he is dispatching a little business, about which he is earnestly employed.

CONSTANCE - He's master of his own occasions. [Exit Servant.

ISABELLA - We shall see him anon, with his face as red as if it had been boiled in pump-water: But, when comes this mirror of knighthood, that is to be presented you for your servant?

CONSTANCE - Oh, 'tis well thought on; 'faith thou know'st my affections are otherwise disposed; he's rich, and thou want'st a fortune; atchieve him, if thou can'st; 'tis but trying, and thou hast as much wit as any wench in England.

ISABELLA - On condition you'll take it for a courtesy to be rid of an ass, I care not if I marry him: the old fool, your father, would be so importunate to match you with a young fool, that, partly for quietness sake, I am content to take him.

CONSTANCE - To take him! then you make sure on't.

ISABELLA - As sure, as if the sack posset were already eaten.

CONSTANCE - But, what means wilt thou use to get him?

ISABELLA - I'll bribe Failer; he's the man.

CONSTANCE - Why, this knight is his inheritance; he lives upon him: Do'st thou think he'll ever admit thee to govern him? No, he fears thy wit too much: Besides, he has already received an hundred pounds, to make the match between Sir Timorous and me.

ISABELLA - 'Tis all one for that; I warrant you, he sells me the fee-simple of him.

SETSTONE - Your father, madam--

Enter NONSUCH.

ISABELLA - The tempest is risen; I see it in his face; he puffs and blows yonder, as if two of the winds were fighting upwards and downwards in his belly.

SETSTONE - Will he not find your false keys, madam?

ISABELLA - I hope he will have more humanity than to search us.

CONSTANCE - You are come after us betimes, sir.

NONSUCH - Oh child! I am undone; I am robbed, I am robbed; I have utterly lost all stomach to my dinner.

CONSTANCE - Robbed! good my lord, how, or of what?

NONSUCH - Two hundred and fifty pounds, in fair gold, out of my study: An hundred of it I was to have paid a courtier this afternoon for a bribe.

SETSTONE - I protest, my lord, I had as much ado to get that parcel of gold for your lordship--

NONSUCH - You must get me as much more against to-morrow; for then my friend at court is to pay his mercer.

ISABELLA - Nay, if that be all, there's no such haste: the courtiers are not so forward to pay their debts.

CONSTANCE - Has not the monkey been in the study? He may have carried it away, and dropt it under the garden-window: the grass is long enough to hide it.

NONSUCH - I'll go see immediately.

Enter FAILER, BURR, TIMOROUS.

FAILER - This is the gentleman, my lord.

NONSUCH - He's welcome.

FAILER - And this the particular of his estate.

NONSUCH - That's welcome too.

FAILER - But, besides the land here mentioned, he has wealth in specie.

NONSUCH - A very fine young gentleman.

TIMOROUS - Now, my lord, I hope there's no great need of wooing: I suppose my estate will speak for me; yet, if you please to put in a word--

NONSUCH - That will I instantly.

TIMOROUS - I hope I shall have your good word, too, madam, to your cousin for me. [To ISABELLA.

ISABELLA - Any thing within my power, Sir Timorous.

NONSUCH - Daughter, here's a person of quality, and one, that loves and honours you exceedingly--

TIMOROUS - Nay, good my lord! you discover all at first dash.

NONSUCH - Let me alone, sir; have not I the dominion over my own daughter? Constance, here's a knight in love with you, child.

CONSTANCE - In love with me, my lord! it is not possible.

NONSUCH - Here he stands, that will make it good, child.

TIMOROUS - Who, I, my lord? I hope her ladyship has a better opinion of me than so.

NONSUCH - What! are not you in love with my daughter? I'll be sworn you told me so but even now: I'll eat words for no man.

TIMOROUS - If your ladyship will believe all reports, that are raised on men of quality--

NONSUCH - He told it me with his own mouth, child: I'll eat words for no man; that's more than ever I told him yet.

FAILER - You told him so but just now; fie, Sir Timorous.

NONSUCH - He shall have no daughter of mine, an he were a thousand knights; he told me, he hoped I would speak for him: I'll eat no man's words; that's more than ever I told him yet.

ISABELLA - You need not keep such a pudder about eating his words; you see he has eaten 'em already for you.

NONSUCH - I'll make him stand to his words, and he shall not marry my daughter neither: By this good day, I will.

[Exit NONSUCH.

CONSTANCE - 'Tis an ill day to him; he has lost two hundred and fifty pounds in't. [To ISABELLA.

BURR - He swears at the rate of two thousand pounds a year, if the Rump act were still in being.

FAILER - He's in passion, man; and, besides, he has been a great fanatic formerly, and now has got a habit of swearing, that he may be thought a cavalier.

BURR - What noise is that? I think I hear your cousin Trice's voice.

FAILER - I'll go see.

[Exit FAILER.

ISABELLA - Come, Sir Timorous, be not discouraged: 'Tis but an old man's frowardness; he's always thus against rain.

Enter FAILER.

FAILER - O madam, follow me quickly; and if you do not see sport, melancholy be upon my head.

[Exuent.

SCENE III

The Scene changes, and TRICE is discovered playing at tables by himself, with spectacles on, a bottle, and parmezan by him; they return and see him, undiscovered by him.

TRICE - Cinque and quatre: My cinque I play here, sir; my quatre here, sir: Now for you, sir: But first I'll drink to you, sir; upon my faith I'll do you reason, sir: Mine was thus full, sir! Pray mind your play, sir:--Size ace I have thrown: I'll play 'em at length, sir.

--Will you, sir? Then you have made a blot sir; I'll try if I can enter: I have hit you, sir.

--I think you can cog a dye, sir.

--I cog a dye, sir? I play as fair as you, or any man.

--You lie, sir.

--How! lie, sir? I'll teach you what 'tis to give a gentleman the lie, sir.

[Throws down the tables.

[They all laugh and discover themselves.

ISABELLA - Is this your serious business?

TRICE - O you rogue, are you there? You are welcome, huswife; and so are you, Constance, Fa tol de re tol de re la. [Claps their backs.

ISABELLA - Pr'ythee be not so rude, Trice.

TRICE - Huswife Constance, I'll have you into my larder, and shew you my provision: I have cockles, dainty fat cockles, that came in the night; if they had seen the day, I would not have given a fart for 'em. I would the king had 'em.

CONSTANCE - He has as good, I warrant you.

TRICE - Nay, that's a lie. I could sit and cry for him sometimes; he does not know what 'tis to eat a good meal in a whole year. His cooks are asses: I have a delicate dish of ruffs to dinner, sirrah.

CONSTANCE - To dinner!

TRICE - To dinner! why by supper they had been past their prime. I'll tell thee the story of 'em: I have a friend--

Enter Servant.

SERVANT -Sir, dinner's upon the table.

TRICE - Well, well; I have a friend, as I told you--

SERVANT - Dinner stays, sir: 'tis dinner that stays: Sure he will hear now.

TRICE - I have a friend, as I told you--

ISABELLA - I believe he's your friend, you are so loth to part with him.

TRICE - Away, away;--I'll tell you the story between the courses. Go you to the cook immediately, sirrah; and bring me word what we have to supper, before we go to dinner: I love to have the satisfaction of the day before me.

[Exuent.

ACT II

SCENE I

Enter, as from Dinner, TRICE, TIMOROUS, FAILER, BURR, CONSTANCE, ISABELLA.

TRICE - Speak thy conscience; was it not well dressed, sirrah?

TIMOROUS - What think you of the Park, after our plenteous entertainment, madam?

ISABELLA - I defy the Park, and all its works.

CONSTANCE - Come, Mr Trice, we'll walk in your garden.

[Exuent all but FAILER and BURR.

FAILER - O, one thing I had almost forgot to tell you; one of us two must ever be near Sir Timorous.

BURR - Why?

FAILER - To guard our interest in him from the enemy, madam Isabella; who, I doubt, has designs upon him. I do not fear her wit, but her sex; she carries a prevailing argument about her.

Enter BIBBER with a Bottle.

BIBBER - By this hand, I have alight upon the best wine in your cousin's cellar; drink but one glass to me, to shew I am welcome, and I am gone.

FAILER - Here then, honest Will; 'tis a cup of forbearance to thee.

BIBBER - Thank you, sir, I'll pledge you--now here's to you again.

FAILER - Come away; what is't, Will?

BIBBER - 'Tis what you christened it, a cup of forbearance, sir.

FAILER - Why, I drank that to thee, Will, that thou shouldst forbear thy money.

BIBBER - And I drink this to you, sir; henceforward I'll forbear working for you.

FAILER - Then say I:
Take a little Bibber,
And threw him in the river;
And if he will trust never,
Then there let him lie ever.

BIBBER - Then say I:
Take a little Failer,
And throw him to the jailor;
And there let him lie,
Till he has paid his tailor.

BURR - You are very smart upon one another, gentlemen.

FAILER - This is nothing between us; I use to tell him of his title, Fiery facias; and his setting dog, that runs into ale-houses before him, and comes questing out again, if any of the woots, his customers, be within.

BIBBER - I'faith 'tis true; and I use to tell him of his two capon's tails about his hat, that are laid spread-eaglewise to make a feather; I would go into the snow at any time, and in a quarter of an hour I would come in with a better feather upon my head; and so farewel, sir; I have had the better on you hitherto, and for this time I am resolved to keep it.

[Exit BIBBER.

FAILER - The rogue's too hard for me; but the best on't is, I have my revenge upon his purse.

Enter ISABELLA.

ISABELLA - Came not Sir Timorous this way, gentlemen? He left us in the garden, and said he would look out my Lord Nonsuch, to make his peace with him.

FAILER - Madam, I like not your enquiring after Sir Timorous: I suspect you have some design upon him: You would fain undermine your cousin, and marry him yourself.

ISABELLA - Suppose I should design it, what are you the worse for my good fortune? Shall I make a proposition to you? I know you two carry a great stroke with him: Make the match between us, and propound to yourselves what advantages you can reasonably hope: You shall chouse him of horses, cloaths, and money, and I'll wink at it.

BURR - And if he will not be choused, shall we beat him out on't?

ISABELLA - For that, as you can agree.

FAILER - Give us a handsel of the bargain; let us enjoy you, and 'tis a match.

ISABELLA - Grammercy i'faith, boys; I love a good offer, howe'er the world goes; but you would not be so base to wrong him that way?

FAILER - I vow to gad but I would, madam: In a horse, or a woman, I may lawfully cheat my own father: Besides, I know the knight's complexion; he would be sure to follow other women; and all that.

ISABELLA - Nay, if he fought with the sword, he should give me leave to fight with the scabbard.

BURR - What say you, madam? Is't a bargain?

ISABELLA - 'Tis but a promise; and I have learnt a court trick for performing any thing [Aside]. Well, gentlemen, when I am married I'll think upon you; you'll grant there's a necessity I should cuckold him, if it were but to prove myself a wit.

FAILER - Nay, there's no doubt you'll cuckold him, and all that; for look you, he's a person fit for nothing else; but I fear we shall not have the graffing of the horns; we must have livery and seisin beforehand of you, or I protest to gad we believe you not.

ISABELLA - I have past my word; is't not sufficient? What! do you think I would tell a lie to save such a paltry thing as a night's lodging?--Hark you, sir. [To BURR.

FAILER - Now will she attempt Burr; egad, she has found him out for the weaker vessel.

ISABELLA - I have no kindness for that Failer; we'll strike him out, and manage Sir Timorous ourselves.

BURR - Indeed we won't.

ISABELLA - Failer's a rook; and, besides, he's such a debauched fellow--

BURR - I am ten times worse.

ISABELLA - Leave it, and him that taught it you: You have virtuous inclinations, and I would not have you ruin yourself. He, that serves many mistresses, surfeits on his diet, and grows dead to the whole sex: 'Tis the folly in the world next long ears and braying.

BURR - Now I'm sure you have a mind to me; when a woman once falls a preaching, the next thing is ever use and application.

ISABELLA - Forbear your rudeness!

BURR - Then I am sure you mean to jilt me: You decline Failer, because he has wit; and you think me such an ass, that you may pack me off so soon as you are married; no, no, I'll not venture certainties for uncertainties.

ISABELLA - I can hold no longer; Mr Failer, what do you think this fellow was saying of you?

FAILER - Of me, madam?

ISABELLA - That you were one of the arrantest cowards in Christendom, though you went for one of the Dear Hearts; that your name had been upon more posts than playbills; and that he had been acquainted with you these seven years, drunk and sober, and yet could never fasten a quarrel upon you.

BURR - Do you believe this, dear heart?

ISABELLA - If you deny it, I'll take his sword, and force you to confess it.

FAILER - I vow to gad; this will not do, madam: You shall not set us at variance so easily; neither shall you have Sir Timorous.

ISABELLA - No! then mark my words: I'll marry him in spite of you; and, which is worse, you shall both work my ends, and I'll discard you for your pains.

FAILER - You shall not touch a bit of him: I'll preserve his humbles from you, egad; they shall be his keeper's fees[A].

[Footnote A: The keeper of a royal forest had for his fees the skin, head, umbles (i.e. inwards), chine, and shoulders. HOLINSHED'S Chronicle, vol. i. p. 104.]

BURR - She shall cut an atom sooner than divide us. [Exeunt BURR and FAILER.

Enter CONSTANCE.

CONSTANCE - I have given 'em the slip in the garden, to come and overhear thee: No fat overgrown virgin of forty ever offered herself so dog-cheap, or was more despised; methinks now this should mortify thee exceedingly.

ISABELLA - Not a whit the more for that: Cousin mine, our sex is not so easily put out of conceit with our own beauties.

CONSTANCE - Thou hast lost the opinion of thy honesty, and got nothing in recompence: Now that's such an oversight in a lady--

ISABELLA - You are deceived; they think me too virtuous for their purpose; but I have yet another way to try, and you shall help me.

Enter LOVEBY, new habited.

CONSTANCE - Mr Loveby, welcome, welcome: Where have you been this fortnight?

LOVEBY - Faith, madam, out of town, to see a little thing that's fallen to me upon the death of a grandmother.

CONSTANCE - You thank death for the windfall, servant: But why are you not in mourning for her?

LOVEBY - Troth, madam, it came upon me so suddenly, I had not time: 'Twas a fortune utterly unexpected by me.

ISABELLA - Why, was your grandmother so young, you could not look for her decease?

LOVEBY - Not for that neither; but I had many other kindred, whom she might have left it to; only she heard I lived here in fashion, and spent my money in the eye of the world.

CONSTANCE - You forge these things prettily; but I have heard you are as poor as a decimated cavalier, and had not one foot of land in all the world.

LOVEBY - Rivals' tales, rivals' tales, madam.

CONSTANCE - Where lies your land, sir?

LOVEBY - I'll tell you, madam, it has upon it a very fair manor house; from one side you have in prospect an hanging garden.

ISABELLA - Who was hanged there? not your grandmother, I hope?

LOVEBY - In the midst of it you have a fountain: You have seen that at Hampton-court? it will serve to give you a slight image of it. Beyond the garden you look to a river through a perspective of fruit-trees; and beyond the river you see a mead so flowery!--Well, I shall never be at quiet, till we two make hay there.

CONSTANCE - But where lies this paradise?

LOVEBY - Pox on't; I am thinking to sell it, it has such a villanous unpleasant name, it would have sounded so harsh in a lady's ear. But for the fountain, madam--

CONSTANCE - The fountain's a poor excuse, it will not hold water; come, the name, the name.

LOVEBY - Faith, it is come so lately into my hands, that I have forgot the name on't.

ISABELLA - That's much, now, that you should forget the name, and yet could make such an exact description of the place.

LOVEBY - If you would needs know, the name's Bawdy.--Sure this will give a stop to their curiosity. [Aside.

ISABELLA - At least you will tell us in what county it lies, that my cousin may send to enquire about it: come, this shall not serve your turn; tell us any town that's near it.

LOVEBY - 'Twill be somewhat too far to send; it lies in the very north of Scotland.

ISABELLA - In good time, a paradise in the Highlands; is't not so, sir?

CONSTANCE - It seems you went post, servant: in troth you are a rank rider, to go to the north of Scotland, stay and take possession, and return again, in ten days time.

ISABELLA - I never knew your grandmother was a Scotch woman: Is she not a Tartar too? Pray whistle for her, and let's see her dance; come--whist, grannee!

CONSTANCE - Fie, fie, servant; what, no invention in you? all this while a-studying for a name of your manor? come, come, where lies it? tell me.

LOVEBY - No, faith, I am wiser than so; I'll discover my seat to no man; so I shall have some damned lawyer keep a prying into my title, to defeat me of it.

CONSTANCE - How then shall I be satisfied, there is such a thing in nature?

LOVEBY - Tell me what jewel you would wear, and you shall have it: Enquire into my money, there's the trial.

CONSTANCE - Since you are so flush, sir, you shall give me a locket of diamonds, of three hundred pounds.

ISABELLA - That was too severe; you know he has but two hundred and fifty pounds to bestow. [To her.

LOVEBY - Well, you shall have it, madam: But I cannot higgle; I know you'll say it did not cost above two hundred pieces.

ISABELLA - I'll be hanged if he does not present you with a parcel of melted flints set in gold, or Norfolk pebbles.

LOVEBY - Little gentlewoman, you are so keen--Madam, this night I have appointed business, to-morrow I'll wait upon you with it.

[Exit LOVEBY.

ISABELLA - By that time he has bought his locket, and paid his landlady, all his money will be gone. But do you mean to prosecute your plot to see him this evening?

CONSTANCE - Yes, and that very privately; if my father know it, I am undone.

Enter SETSTONE.

ISABELLA - I heard him say, this night he had appointed business.

SETSTONE - Why, that was it, madam; according to your order, I put on a disguise, and found him in the Temple-walks: Having drawn him aside, I told him, if he expected happiness, he must meet me in a blind alley, I nam'd to him, on the back side of Mr Trice's house, just at the close of evening; there he should be satisfied from whom he had his supplies of money.

CONSTANCE - And how did he receive the summons?

SETSTONE - Like a bold Hector of Troy; without the least doubt or scruple: But, the jest on't was, he would needs believe that I was the devil.

CONSTANCE - Sure he was afraid to come then?

SETSTONE - Quite contrary; he told me I need not be so shy, to acknowledge myself to him; he knew I was the devil; but he had learnt so much civility, as not to press his friend to a farther discovery than he was pleased. I should see I had to do with a gentleman; and any courtesy I should confer on him, he would not be unthankful; for he hated ingratitude of all things.

CONSTANCE - 'Twas well carried not to disabuse him: I laugh to think what sport I shall have anon, when I convince him of his lies, and let him know I was the devil, to whom he was beholden for his money: Go, Setstone; and in the same disguise be ready for him. [Exit SETSTONE.

ISABELLA - How dare you trust this fellow?

CONSTANCE - I must trust some body: Gain has made him mine, and now fear will keep him faithful.

To them, BURR, FAILER, TIMOROUS, TRICE, and NONSUCH.

FAILER - Pray, my lord, take no pique at it: 'Tis not given to all men to be confident: Egad, you shall see Sir Timorous will redeem all upon the next occasion.

NONSUCH - A raw miching boy.

ISABELLA - And what are you but an old boy of five and fifty? I never knew any thing so humoursome--I warrant you, Sir Timorous; I'll speak for you.

NONSUCH - Would'st thou have me be friends with him? for thy sake he shall only add five hundred a-year to her jointure, and I'll be satisfied: Come you hither, sir.

[Here TRICE and NONSUCH and TIMOROUS talk privately; BURR with FAILER apart, CONSTANCE with ISABELLA.

CONSTANCE - You'll not find your account in this trick to get Failer beaten; 'tis too palpable and open.

ISABELLA - I warrant you 'twill pass upon Burr for a time: So my revenge and your interest will go on together.

FAILER - Burr, there's mischief a-brewing, I know it by their whispering, I vow to gad: Look to yourself, their design is on you; for my part, I am a person that am above 'em.

TIMOROUS - [To Trice] But then you must speak for me, Mr Trice and you too, my lord.

NONSUCH - If you deny't again, I'll beat you; look to't, boy.

TRICE - Come on; I'll make the bargain.

ISABELLA - You were ever good in a flesh-market.

TRICE - Come, you little harlotry; what satisfaction can you give me for running away before the ruffs came in?

CONSTANCE - Why, I left you to 'em, that ever invite your own belly to the greatest part of all your feasts.

TRICE - I have brought you a knight here, huswife, with a plentiful fortune to furnish out a table; and what would you more? Would you be an angel in heaven?

ISABELLA - Your mind's ever upon your belly.

TRICE - No: 'tis sometimes upon yours: But, what say'st thou to sir Timorous, little Constance?

CONSTANCE - Would you have me married to that king Midas's face?

TRICE - Midas me no Midas; he's a wit; he understands eating and drinking well: Poeta coquus, the heathen philosopher could tell you that.

CONSTANCE - Come on, sir: what's your will with me? [Laughs.

TIMOROUS - Why, madam, I could only wish we were a little better acquainted, that we might not laugh at one another so.

CONSTANCE - If the fool puts forward, I am undone.

TIMOROUS - Fool!--do you know me, madam?

CONSTANCE - You may see I know you, because I call you by your name.

FAILER - You must endure these rebukes with patience, Sir Timorous.

CONSTANCE - What, are you planet struck? Look you, my lord, the gentleman's tongue-tied.

NONSUCH - This is past enduring.

FAILER - 'Tis nothing, my lord;--courage, Sir Timorous.

NONSUCH - I say 'tis past enduring; that's more than ever I told you yet: Do you come to make a fool of my daughter?

ISABELLA - Why lord--

NONSUCH - Why lady [Exit NONSUCH.

TRICE - Let's follow the old man, and pacify him.

ISABELLA - Now, cousin, [Exuent ISABELLA, TRICE, BURR.

CONSTANCE - Well, Mr Failer, I did not think you, of all the rest, would have endeavoured a thing so much against my inclination, as this marriage: if you had been acquainted with my heart, I am sure you would not.

FAILER - What can the meaning of this be? you would not have me believe you love me; and yet how otherwise to understand you I vow to gad I cannot comprehend.

CONSTANCE - I did not say I loved you; but if I should take a fancy to your person and humour, I hope it is no crime to tell it you. Women are tied to hard unequal laws: The passion is the same in us, and yet we are debarred the freedom to express it. You make poor Grecian beggars of us ladies; our desires must have no language, but only be fastened to our breasts.

FAILER - Come, come; egad I know the whole sex of you: Your love's at best but a kind: of blind-man's-buff, catching at him that's next in your way.

CONSTANCE - Well, sir, I can take nothing ill from you; when 'tis too late you'll see how unjust you have been to me. I have said too much already.--[Is going.

FAILER - Nay stay, sweet madam! I vow to gad my fortune's better than I could imagine.

CONSTANCE - No, pray let me go, sir; perhaps I was in jest.

FAILER - Really, madam, I look upon you as a person of such worth, and all that, that I vow to gad I honour you of all persons in the world; and though I am a person that am inconsiderable in the world, and all that, madam, for a person of your worth and excellency I would--

CONSTANCE - What would you, sir?

FAILER - Sacrifice my life and fortunes, I vow to gad, madam.

Enter ISABELLA, BURR, and TIMOROUS, at a distance from them.

ISABELLA - There's Failer close in talk with my cousin; he's soliciting your suit, I warrant you, Sir Timorous: Do but observe with what passion he courts for you.

BURR - I do not like that kneading of her hand though.

ISABELLA - Come, you are such a jealous coxcomb: I warrant you suspect there's some amour between 'em; there can be nothing in't, it is so open: Pray observe.

BURR - But how come you so officious, madam? you, that ere now had a design upon Sir Timorous for yourself?

ISABELLA - I thought you had a better opinion of my wit, than to think I was in earnest. My cousin may do what she pleases, but he shall never pin himself upon me, assure him.

CONSTANCE – [To FAILER] Sir Timorous little knows how dangerous a person he has employed in making love. [Aloud.

BURR - How's this! Pray, my lady Constance, what's the meaning of that you say to Failer?

FAILER - What luck was this, that he should overhear you! Pax on't!

CONSTANCE - Mr Burr, I owe you not that satisfaction; what you have heard you may interpret as you please.

TIMOROUS - The rascal has betrayed me.

ISABELLA - In earnest, sir, I do not like it.

FAILER - Dear Mr Burr, be pacified; you are a person I have an honour for; and this change of affairs shall not be the worse for you, egad, sir.

CONSTANCE - Bear up resolutely, Mr Failer; and maintain my favours, as becomes my servant.

BURR - He maintain 'em! go, you Judas; I'll teach you what 'tis to play fast and loose with a man of war. [Kicks him.

TIMOROUS - Lay it on, Burr.

ISABELLA - Spare him not, Burr.

CONSTANCE - Fear him not, servant.

FAILER - Oh, oh! would nobody were on my side! here I am praised, I vow to gad, into all the colours of the rainbow.

CONSTANCE - But remember 'tis for me.

BURR - As you like this, proceed, sir; but, come not near me to-night, while I'm in wrath.

[Exeunt BURR and TIMOROUS.

CONSTANCE - Come, sir; how fare you after your sore trial? You bore it with a most heroic patience.

ISABELLA - Brave man at arms, but weak to Balthazar[A]!

[Footnote A: Alluding to the old play of Hieronymo.]

FAILER - I hope to gad, madam, you'll consider the merit of my sufferings. I would not have been beaten thus, but to obey that person in the world--

CONSTANCE - Heaven reward you for't; I never shall.

FAILER - How, madam!

ISABELLA - Art thou such an ass, as not to perceive thou art abused? This beating I contrived for you: you know upon what account; and have yet another or two at your service. Yield up the knight in time, 'tis your best course.

FAILER - Then does not your ladyship love me, madam?

CONSTANCE - Yes, yes, I love to see you beaten.

ISABELLA - Well, methinks now you have had a hard bargain on't: You have lost your cully, Sir Timorous, and your friend, Burr, and all to get a poor beating. But I'll see it mended against next time for you.

[Exeunt CONSTANCE and ISABELLA, laughing.

FAILER - I am so much amazed, I vow to gad, I do not understand my own condition. [Exit.

SCENE II

Enter LOVEBY solus, in the dark, his sword drawn, groping out his way.

LOVEBY - This is the time and place he pointed me, and 'tis certainly the devil I am to meet; for no mortal creature could have that kindness for me, to supply my necessities as he has done, nor could have done it in so strange a manner. He told me he was a scholar, and had been a parson in the fanatic's times: a shrewd suspicion it was the devil; or at least a limb of him. If the devil can send churchmen on his errands, lord have mercy on the laity! Well, let every man speak as he finds, and give the devil his due; I think him a very honest and well-natured fellow; and if I hear any man speak ill of him, except it be a parson, that gets his living by it, I wear a sword at his service. Yet, for all this, I do not much care to see him. He does not mean to hook me in for my soul, does he? If he does, I shall desire to be excused. But what a rogue am I, to suspect a person, that has dealt so much like a gentleman by me! He comes to bring me money, and would do it handsomely, that it might not be perceived. Let it be as 'twill, I'll seem to trust him; and, then, if he have any thing of a gentleman in him, he wills corn to deceive me, as much as I would to cozen him, if I were the devil, and he Jack Loveby.

Enter FAILER at the other end of the stage.

FAILER - What will become of me to-night! I am just in the condition of an out-lying deer, that's beaten from his walk for offering to rut. Enter I dare not, for Burr.

LOVEBY - I hear a voice, but nothing do I see. Speak, what thou art?

FAILER - There he is, watching for me. I must venture to run by him; and, when I am in, I hope my cousin Trice will defend me. The devil would not lie abroad in such a night.

LOVEBY - I thought it was the devil, before he named himself.

[FAILER goes to run off, and falls into LOVEBY'S arms.

LOVEBY - Honest Satan, well encountered! I am sorry, with all my heart, it is so dark. 'Faith, I should be very glad to see thee at my lodging; pr'ythee, let's not be such strangers to one another for the time to come. And what hast thou got under thy cloak there, little Satan? I warrant thou hast brought me some more money.

FAILER - Help, help; thieves! thieves!

[LOVEBY lets him go.

LOVEBY - This is Failer's voice: How the devil was I mistaken! I must get off, ere company comes in.

[Exit Loveby.

FAILER - Thieves! thieves!

Enter Trice, Burr, and Timorous, undressed.

ALL - Where! where!

FAILER - One was here just now; and it should be Loveby by his voice, but I have no witness.

TRICE - It cannot be; he wants no money.

BURR - Come, sirrah; I'll take pity on you to-night: You shall lie in the truckle-bed.

TRICE - Pox o' this noise! it has disturbed me from such a dream of eating!--[Exeunt.

SCENE I

Enter CONSTANCE and ISABELLA.

CONSTANCE - Twas ill luck to have the meeting broke last night, just as Setstone was coming towards him.

ISABELLA - But, in part of recompence, you'll have the pleasure of putting him on farther straits. O, these little mischiefs are meat and drink to me.

CONSTANCE - He shall tell me from whence he has his money: I am resolved now to try him to the utmost.

ISABELLA - I would devise something for him to do, which he could not possibly perform.

CONSTANCE - As I live, yonder he comes, with the jewel in his hand he promised me. Pr'ythee, leave me alone with him.

ISABELLA - Speed the plough! If I can make no sport, I'll hinder none. I'll to my knight, Sir Timorous; shortly you shall hear news from Dametas[A]. [Footnote A: A foolish character in Sir Philip Sidney's Arcadia, who seems to have become proverbial.]

[Exit ISABELLA.

Enter LOVEBY.

LOVEBY - Look you, madam, here's the jewel; do me the favour to accept it, and suppose a very good compliment delivered with it.

CONSTANCE - Believe me, a very fair jewel. But why will you be at this needless charge? What acknowledgment do you expect? You know I will not marry you.

LOVEBY - How the devil do I know that? I do not conceive myself, under correction, so inconsiderable a person.

CONSTANCE - You'll alter your partial opinion, when I tell you, 'tis not a flash of wit fires me, nor is it a gay out-side can seduce me to matrimony.

LOVEBY - I am neither fool, nor deformed, so much as to be despicable. What do I want?

CONSTANCE - A good estate, that makes every thing handsome: Nothing can look well without it.

LOVEBY - Does this jewel express poverty?

CONSTANCE - I conjure you by your love to me, tell me one truth not minced by your invention, how came you by this jewel?

LOVEBY - 'Tis well I have a voucher. Pray ask your own jeweller, Setstone, if I did not buy it of him.

CONSTANCE - How glad you are now, you can tell a truth so near a lie. But where had you the money, that purchased it? Come--without circumstances and preambles--

LOVEBY - Umph--Perhaps, that may be a secret.

CONSTANCE - Say, it be one; yet he, that loved indeed, could not keep it from his mistress.

LOVEBY - Why should you be thus importunate?

CONSTANCE - Because I cannot think you love me, if you will not trust that to my knowledge, which you conceal from all the world beside.

LOVEBY - You urge me deeply--

CONSTANCE - Come, sweet servant, you shall tell me; I am resolved to take no denial. Why do you sigh?

LOVEBY - If I be blasted, it must out.

CONSTANCE - Either tell me, or resolve to take your leave for ever.

LOVEBY - Then know, I have my means,--I know not how.

CONSTANCE - This is a fine secret.

LOVEBY - Why, then, if you will needs know, 'tis from the devil; I have money from him, what, and when I please.

CONSTANCE - Have you sealed a covenant, and given away your soul for money?

LOVEBY - No such thing intended on my part.

CONSTANCE - How then?

LOVEBY - I know not yet what conditions he'll propose. I should have spoke with him last night, but that a cross chance hindered it.

CONSTANCE - Well, my opinion is, some great lady, that is in love with you, supplies you still; and you tell me an incredible tale of the devil, merely to shadow your infidelity.

LOVEBY - Devise some means to try me.

CONSTANCE - I take you at your word. You shall swear freely to bestow on me whatever you shall gain this unknown way; and, for a proof, because you tell me you can have money, what, and when you please, bring me a hundred pounds ere night.--If I do marry him for a wit, I'll see what he can do; he shall have none from me. [Aside.

LOVEBY - You overjoy me, madam; you shall have it, an 'twere twice as much.

CONSTANCE - How's this?

LOVEBY - The devil a cross that I have, or know where to get; but I must promise well, to save my credit.--Now, devil, if thou dost forsake me!

[Aside.

CONSTANCE - I mistrust you; and, therefore, if you fail, I'll have your hand to show against you; here's ink and paper. [LOVEBY writes.

Enter BURR, and TIMOROUS.

BURR - What makes Loveby yonder? He's writing somewhat.

TIMOROUS - I'll go see. [Looks over him.

LOVEBY - Have you no more manners than to overlook a man when he's a writing?--Oh! is't you, Sir Timorous? You may stand still; now I think on't, you cannot read written hand.

BURR - You are very familiar with Sir Timorous.

LOVEBY - So am I with his companions, sir.

BURR - Then there's hopes you and I may be better acquainted. I am one of his companions.

LOVEBY - By what title? as you are an ass, sir?

CONSTANCE - No more, Loveby.

LOVEBY - I need not, madam. Alas! this fellow is only the solicitor of a quarrel, 'till he has brought it to an head; and will leave the fighting part to the courteous pledger. Do not I know these fellows? You shall as soon persuade a mastiff to fasten on a lion, as one of those to engage with a courage above their own: They know well enough whom they can beat, and who can beat them.

Enter FAILER at a distance.

FAILER - Yonder they are: Now, would I compound for a reasonable sum, that I were friends with Burr. If I am not, I shall lose Sir Timorous.

CONSTANCE - O, servant, have I spied you? let me run into your arms.

FAILER - I renounce my lady Constance: I vow to gad, I renounce her.

TIMOROUS - To your task, Burr.

Enter NONSUCH and ISABELLA.

CONSTANCE - Hold, gentlemen! no sign of quarrel.

NONSUCH - O, friends! I think I shall go mad with grief: I have lost more money.

LOVEBY - Would I had it: that's all the harm I wish myself. Your servant, madam; I go about the business.

Exit LOVEBY.

NONSUCH - What! does he take no pity on me?

CONSTANCE - Pr'ythee, moan him, Isabella.

ISABELLA - Alas, alas, poor uncle! could they find in their hearts to rob him!

NONSUCH - Five hundred pounds, out of poor six thousand pounds a-year! I, and mine, are undone for ever.

FAILER - Your own house, you think, is clear, my lord?

CONSTANCE - I dare answer for all there, as much as for myself.

BURR - Oh, that he would but think that Loveby had it!

FAILER - If you'll be friends with me, I'll try what I can persuade him to.

BURR - Here's my hand, I will, dear heart.

FAILER - Your own house being clear, my lord, I am apt to suspect this Loveby for such a person. Did you mark how abruptly he went out?

NONSUCH - He did indeed, Mr Failer. But why should I suspect him? his carriage is fair, and his means great; he could never live after this rate, if it were not.

FAILER - This still renders him the more suspicious: He has no land, to my knowledge.

BURR - Well said, mischief. [Aside.

CONSTANCE - My father's credulous, and this rogue has found the blind side of him; would Loveby heard him! [To ISABELLA.

FAILER - He has no means, and he loses at play; so that, for my part, I protest to gad, I am resolved he picks locks for his living.

BURR - Nay, to my knowledge, he picks locks.

TIMOROUS - And to mine.

FAILER - No longer ago than last night he met me in the dark, and offered to dive into my pockets.

NONSUCH - That's a main argument for suspicion.

FAILER - I remember once, when the keys of the Exchequer were lost in the Rump-time, he was sent for upon an extremity, and, egad, he opens me all the locks with the blade-bone of a breast of mutton.

NONSUCH - Who, this Loveby?

FAILER - This very Loveby. Another time, when we had sate up very late at ombre in the country, and were hungry towards morning, he plucks me out (I vow to gad I tell you no lie) four ten-penny nails from the dairy lock with his teeth, fetches me out a mess of milk, and knocks me 'em in again with his head, upon reputation.

ISABELLA - Thou boy!

NONSUCH - What shall I do in this case? My comfort is, my gold's all marked.

CONSTANCE - Will you suspect a gentleman of Loveby's worth, upon the bare report of such a rascal as this Failer?

NONSUCH - Hold thy tongue, I charge thee; upon my blessing hold thy tongue. I'll have him apprehended before he sleeps; come along with me, Mr Failer.

FAILER - Burr, look well to Sir Timorous; I'll be with you instantly.

CONSTANCE - I'll watch you by your favour. [Aside.

[Exeunt NONSUCH and FAILER, CONSTANCE following them.

ISABELLA - A word, Sir Timorous.

BURR - [Gets behind.] She shall have a course at the knight, and come up to him, but when she is just ready to pinch, he shall give such a loose from her, shall break her heart.

ISABELLA - Burr there still, and watching us? There's certainly some plot in this, but I'll turn it to my own advantage. [Aside.

TIMOROUS - Did you mark Burr's retirement, madam?

ISABELLA - Ay; his guilt, it seems, makes him shun your company.

TIMOROUS - In what can he be guilty?

ISABELLA - You must needs know it; he courts your mistress.

TIMOROUS - Is he, too, in love with my lady Constance?

ISABELLA - No, no: but, which is worse, he courts me.

TIMOROUS - Why, what have I to do with you? You know I care not this for you.

ISABELLA - Perhaps so; but he thought you did: and good reason for it.

TIMOROUS - What reason, madam?

ISABELLA - The most convincing in the world: He knew my cousin Constance never loved you: He has heard her say, you were as invincibly ignorant as a town-fop judging a new play: as shame-faced as a great overgrown school-boy: in fine, good for nothing but to be wormed out of your estate, and sacrificed to the god of laughter.

TIMOROUS - Was your cousin so barbarous to say this?

ISABELLA - In his hearing.

TIMOROUS - And would he let me proceed in my suit to her?

ISABELLA - For that I must excuse him; he never thought you could love one of my cousin's humour; but took your court to her, only as a blind to your affection for me; and, being possessed with that opinion, he thought himself as worthy as you to marry me.

TIMOROUS - He is not half so worthy; and so I'll tell him, in a fair way.

BURR - [To a Boy entering.] Sirrah, boy, deliver this note to madam Isabella; but be not known I am so near.

BOY - I warrant you, sir.

BURR - Now, Fortune, all I desire of thee is, that Sir Timorous may see it; if he once be brought to believe there is a kindness between her and me, it will ruin all her projects.

ISABELLA - [To the Boy.] From whom?

BOY - From Mr Burr, madam.

ISABELLA - [Reads.] These for Madam Isabella. Dear rogue, Sir Timorous knows nothing of our kindness, nor shall for me; seem still to have designs upon him; it will hide thy affection the better to thy servant, BURR.

ISABELLA - Alas, poor woodcock, dost thou go a-birding? Thou hast e'en set a springe to catch thy own neck. Look you here, Sir Timorous; here's something to confirm what I have told you. [Gives him the letter.

TIMOROUS - D, e, a, r, dear; r, o, g, u, e, rogue. Pray, madam, read it; this written hand is such a damned pedantic thing, I could never away with it.

ISABELLA - He would fain have robbed you of me: Lord, Lord! to see the malice of a man.

TIMOROUS - She has persuaded me so damnably, that I begin to think she's my mistress indeed.

ISABELLA - Your mistress? why, I hope you are not to doubt that, at this time of day. I was your mistress from the first day you ever saw me.

TIMOROUS - Nay, like enough you were so; but I vow to gad now, I was wholly ignorant of my own affection.

ISABELLA - And this rogue pretends he has an interest in me, merely to defeat you: Look you, look you, where he stands in ambush, like a Jesuit behind a Quaker, to see how his design will take.

TIMOROUS - I see the rogue: Now could I find in my heart to marry you in spite to him; what think you on't, in a fair way?

ISABELLA - I have brought him about as I could wish; and now I'll make my own conditions. [Aside.] Sir Timorous, I wish you well; but he I marry must promise me to live at London: I cannot abide to be in the country, like a wild beast in the wilderness, with no Christian soul about me.

TIMOROUS - Why, I'll bear you company.

ISABELLA - I cannot endure your early hunting-matches there; to have my sleep disturbed by break of day, with heigh, Jowler, Jowler! there Venus, ah Beauty! and then a serenade of deep-mouthed curs, to answer the salutation of the huntsman, as if hell were broke loose about me: and all this to meet a pack of gentlemen savages, to ride all day, like mad-men, for the immortal fame of being first in at the hare's death: to come upon the spur, after a trial at four in the afternoon, to destruction of cold meat and cheese, with your lewd company in boots; fall a-drinking till supper time, be carried to bed, tossed out of your cellar, and be good for nothing all the night after.

TIMOROUS - Well, madam, what is it you would be at? you shall find me reasonable to all your propositions.

ISABELLA - I have but one condition more to add; for I will be as reasonable as you; and that is a very poor request--to have all the money in my disposing.

TIMOROUS - How, all the money?

ISABELLA - Ay, for I am sure I can huswife it better for your honour; not but that I shall be willing to encourage you with pocket-money, or so, sometimes.

TIMOROUS - This is somewhat hard.

ISABELLA - Nay, if a woman cannot do that, I shall think you have an ill opinion of my virtue: Not trust your own flesh and blood, Sir Timorous?

TIMOROUS - Well, is there any thing more behind?

ISABELLA - Nothing more, only the choice of my own company, my own hours, and my own actions: These trifles granted me, in all things of moment, I am your most obedient wife and servant, Isabella.

TIMOROUS - Is't a match, then?

ISABELLA - For once I am content it shall; but 'tis to redeem you from those rascals, Burr and Failer-- that way, Sir Timorous, for fear of spies; I'll meet you at the garden door.--[Exit TIMOROUS.] I have led all women the way, if they dare but follow me.

And now march off, if I can scape but spying,
With my drums beating, and my colours flying

[Exit.

BURR - So, their wooing's at an end; thanks to my wit.

Enter FAILER.

FAILER - O Burr! whither is it Sir Timorous and Madam Isabella are gone together?

BURR - Adore my wit, boy; they are parted, never to meet again.

FAILER - I saw them meet just now at the garden-door: So ho, ho, ho, who's within there! Help here quickly, quickly.

Enter NONSUCH and two Servants.

NONSUCH - What's the matter?

FAILER - Your niece Isabella has stolen away Sir Timorous.

NONSUCH - Which way took they?

FAILER - Follow me, I'll show you.

NONSUCH - Break your necks after him, you idle varlets.

[Exeunt.

SCENE II

Enter LOVEBY. LOVEBY'S collar unbuttoned, band carelessly on, hat on the table, as new risen from sleep.

LOVEBY - Boy! how long have I slept, boy?

Enter Boy.

BOY - Two hours and a half, sir.

LOVEBY - What's a-clock, sirrah?

BOY - Near four, sir.

LOVEBY - Why, there's it: I have promised my lady Constance an hundred pounds ere night; I had four hours to perform it in, when I engaged to do it; and I have slept out more than two of them. All my hope to get this money lies within the compass of that hat there. Before I lay down, I made bold a little to prick my finger, and write a note, in the blood of it, to this same friend of mine in t'other world, that uses to supply me: the devil has now had above two hours to perform it in; all which time I have slept, to give him the better opportunity: time enough for a gentleman of his agility to fetch it from the East Indies, out of one of his temples where they worship him; or, if he were lazy, and not minded to go so far, 'twere but stepping over sea, and borrowing so much money out of his own bank at Amsterdam: hang it, what's an hundred pounds between him and me? Now does my heart go pit-a-pat, for fear I should not find the money there: I would fain lift it up to see, and yet I am so afraid of missing: Yet a plague, why should I fear he'll fail me; the name of a friend's a sacred thing; sure he'll consider that. Methinks, this hat looks as if it should have something under it: If one could see the yellow boys peeping underneath the brims now: Ha! [Looks under round about.] In my conscience I think I do. Stand out o'the way, sirrah, and be ready to gather up the pieces, that will flush out of the hat as I take it up.

BOY - What, is my master mad, trow?

[LOVEBY snatches up the hat, looks in it hastily, and sees nothing but the paper.

LOVEBY - Now, the devil take the devil! A plague! was ever man served so as I am! [Throws his hat upon the ground.] To break the bands of amity for one hundred pieces! Well, it shall be more out of thy way than thou imaginest, devil: I'll turn parson, and be at open defiance with thee: I'll lay the wickedness of all people upon thee, though thou art never so innocent; I'll convert thy bawds and whores; I'll Hector thy gamesters, that they shall not dare to swear, curse, or bubble; nay, I'll set thee out so, that thy very usurers and aldermen shall fear to have to do with thee.

[A noise within of ISABELLA and FRANCES.

Enter FRANCES, thrusting back ISABELLA and TIMOROUS.

FRANCES - How now, what's the matter?

ISABELLA - Nay, sweet mistress, be not so hard-hearted; all I desire of you is but harbour for a minute: you cannot, in humanity, deny that small succour to a gentlewoman.

FRANCES - A gentlewoman! I thought so; my house, affords no harbour for gentlewomen: you are a company of proud harlotries: I'll teach you to take place of tradesmen's wives, with a wannion to you.

LOVEBY - How's this! Madam Isabella!

ISABELLA - Mr Loveby! how happy am I to meet with you in my distress!

LOVEBY - What's the matter, madam?

ISABELLA - I'll tell you, if this gentlewoman will give me leave.

FRANCES - No, gentlewoman, I will not give you leave; they are such as we maintain your pride, as they say. [ISABELLA and LOVEBY whisper.] Our husbands trust you, and you must go before their wives. I am sure my good-man never goes to any of your lodgings, but he comes home the worse for it, as they say.

LOVEBY - Is that all? pr'ythee, good landlady, for my sake entertain my friends.

FRANCES - If the gentleman's worship had come alone, it may be I might have entertained him; but for your minion!

Enter NONSUCH, FAILER, BURR, and Officers. Cry within, Here, here.

FAILER - My lord, arrest Sir Timorous upon a promise of marriage to your daughter, and we'll witness it.

TIMOROUS - Why, what a strange thing of you's this, madam Isabella, to bring a man into trouble thus!

FAILER - You are not yet married to her?

TIMOROUS - Not that I remember.

ISABELLA - Well, Failer, I shall find a time to reward your diligence.

LOVEBY - If the knight would have owned his action, I should have taught some of you more manners, than to come with officers into my lodging.

FRANCES - I'm glad with all my heart this minx is prevented of her design: the gentleman had got a great catch of her, as they say. His old father in the country would have given him but little thanks for it, to see him bring down a fine-bred woman, with a lute, and a dressing-box, and a handful of money to her portion.

ISABELLA - Good Mistress Whatdeelack! I know your quarrel to the ladies; do they take up the gallants from the tradesmen's wives? Lord, what a grievous thing it is, for a she citizen to be forced to have children by her own husband!

FRANCES - Come, come, you're a slanderful huswife, and I squorn your harlotry tricks, that I do, so I do.

ISABELLA - Steeple-hat your husband never gets a good look when he comes home, except he brings a gentleman to dinner; who, if he casts an amorous eye towards you, then, "Trust him, good husband, sweet husband, trust him for my sake: Verily the gentleman's an honest man, I read it in his countenance: and if you should not be at home to receive the money, I know he will pay the debt to me." Is't not so, mistress?

Enter BIBBER in slippers, with a skein of silk about his neck.

FRANCES - Will you see me wronged thus, under my own roof, as they say, William?

ISABELLA - Nay, 'tis very true, mistress: you let the men, with old compliments, take up new clothes; I do not mean your wife's clothes, Mr Merchant-Tailor.

BIBBER - Good, i'faith! a notable smart gentlewoman!

ISABELLA - Look to your wife, sir, or, in time, she may undo your trade; for she'll get all your men-customers to herself.

BIBBER - An' I should be hanged, I can forbear no longer. [He plucks out his measure, and runs to ISABELLA, to take measure of her.

ISABELLA - How now! what means Prince Pericles by this?

BIBBER - [On his knees.] I must beg your ladyship e'en to have the honour to trust you but for your gown, for the sake of that last jest, flowered sattin, wrought tabby, silver upon any grounds; I shall run mad if I may not trust your ladyship.

FRANCES - I think you are mad already, as they say, William: You shall not trust her--

[Plucks him back.

BIBBER - Let me alone, Frances: I am a lion when I am angered.

ISABELLA - Pray do not pull your lion by the tail so, mistress--In these clothes, that he now takes measure of me for, will I marry Sir Timorous; mark that, and tremble, Failer.

FAILER - Never threaten me, madam; you're a person I despise.

ISABELLA - I vow to gad, I'll be even with you, sir.

[Exit.

NONSUCH - [To the Bailiffs.]--And when you have arrested him, be sure you search him for my gold.

BAILIFF - [To LOVEBY.] We arrest you, sir, at my Lord Nonsuch's suit.

LOVEBY - Me, you rascals!

NONSUCH - Search him for my gold; you know the marks on't.

LOVEBY - If they can find any marked or unmarked gold about me, they'll find more than I can. You expect I should resist now; no, no; I'll hamper you for this.

BAILIFF -There's nothing to be found about him.

FAILER - 'Tis no matter, to prison with him; there all his debts will come upon him.

LOVEBY - What, hurried to durance, like a stinkard!

FAILER - Now, as I live, a pleasant gentleman; I could find in my heart to bail him; but I'll overcome myself, and steal away. [Is going.

BAILIFF - Come, sir, we must provide you of another lodging; but I believe you'll scarce like it.

LOVEBY - If I do not, I ask no favour; pray turn me out of doors.

BIBBER - Turn him out of doors! What a jest was there? Now, an' I should be hanged, I cannot forbear bailing him: Stay, officers, I bail him body and soul for that jest.

FAILER - Let us begone in time, Burr.

[Exuent BURR, FAILER, and TIMOROUS.

FRANCES - You shall not bail him.

BIBBER - I know I am a rogue to do it; but his wit has prevailed upon me, and a man must not go against his conscience. There, officers.

LOVEBY - to NONSUCH - Old man, if it were not for thy daughter--

NONSUCH - Well, well; take your course, sir.

[Exuent NONSUCH and Bailiffs.

LOVEBY - Come, Will, I'll thank thee at the tavern. Frances, remember this the next time you come up to make my bed.

FRANCES - Do your worst, I fear you not, sir. This is twice to day, William; to trust a gentlewoman, and bail a ragamuffin: I am sure he called you cuckold but yesterday, and said he would make you one.

LOVEBY - Look you, Frances, I am a man of honour, and, if I said it, I'll not break my word with you.

BIBBER - There he was with you again, Frances: An excellent good jest, i'faith la.

FRANCES - I'll not endure it, that I won't, so I won't: I'll go to the justice's worship, and fetch a warrant for him.

LOVEBY - But, landlady, the word cuckold will bear no action in the law, except you could prove your husband prejudiced by it. Have any of his customers forsook him for't? Or any mercer refused to trust him the less, for my calling him so?

FRANCES - Nay, I know not for the mercers; perhaps the citizens may take it for no slander among one another, as they say: but for the gentlemen--

LOVEBY - Will, have they forsaken thee upon it?

BIBBER - No, I assure you, sir.

LOVEBY - No, I warrant 'em: A cuckold has the signification of an honest well-meaning citizen; one, that is not given to jealousies or suspicions; a just person to his wife, &c.; one that, to speak the worst of him, does but to her, what he would be content should be done to her by other men.

FRANCES - But that another man should be the father of his children, as they say; I don't think that a civil thing, husband.

LOVEBY - Not civil, landlady! why all things are civil, that are made so by custom.

BIBBER - Why may not he get as fine children as I, or any man?

FRANCES - But if those children, that are none of yours, should call you father, William!

BIBBER - If they call me father, and are none of mine, I am the more beholden to 'em.

FRANCES - Nay, if that be your humour, husband, I am glad I know it, that I may please you the better another time, as they say.

[Exit FRANCES.

BIBBER - Nay, but Frances, Frances! 'tis such another woman.

[Exit BIBBER.

LOVEBY - 'Tis such another man:--My coat and sword, boy, I must go to Justice Trice's; bring the women; and come after me.

[Exit LOVEBY.

ACT IV

SCENE I

A Table set with Cards upon it.

TRICE walking: Enter Servant.

SERVANT - Sir, some company is without upon justice-business.

TRICE - Saucy rascal, to disturb my meditations. [Exit Servant.--Ay, it shall be he: Jack Loveby, what think'st thou of a game at piquet, we two, hand to fist? you and I will play one single game for ten pieces: 'Tis deep stake, Jack, but 'tis all one between us two: You shall deal, Jack: Who I, Mr Justice! that's a good one; you must give me use for your hand then; that's six i'the hundred. Come, lift, lift; mine's a ten; Mr Justice: mine's a king; oh ho, Jack, you deal. I have the advantage of this, i'faith, if I can keep it. [He deals twelve a piece, two by two, and looks on his own cards.] I take seven, and look on this--Now for you, Jack Loveby.

Enter LOVEBY behind.

LOVEBY - How's this? Am I the man he fights with?

TRICE - I'll do you right, Jack; as I am an honest man, you must discard this; there's no other way: If you were my own brother, I could do no better for you.--Zounds, the rogue has a quint-major, and three aces younger hand.--[Looks on the other cards.] Stay; what am I for the point? But bare forty, and he fifty-one: Fifteen, and five for the point, twenty, and three by aces, twenty-three; well, I am to play first: one, twenty-three; two, twenty-three; three, twenty-three; four, twenty-three;--Pox on't, now I must play into his hand: five:--now you take it, Jack;--five, twenty-four, twenty-five, twenty-six, twenty-seven, twenty-eight, twenty-nine, thirty, and the cards forty.

LOVEBY - Hitherto it goes well on my side.--

TRICE - Now I deal: How many do you take, Jack? All. Then I am gone: What a rise is here! Fourteen by aces, and a sixieme-major; I am gone, without looking into my cards.--[Takes up an ace and bites it.] Ay, I thought so: If ever man play'd with such cursed fortune, I'll be hanged, and all for want of this damned ace--there's your ten pieces, with a pox to you, for a rooking beggarly rascal as you are.

LOVEBY enters.

LOVEBY - What occasion have I given you for these words, sir? Rook and rascal! I am no more rascal than yourself, sir.

TRICE - How's this! how's this!

LOVEBY - And though for this time I put up, because I am a winner-- [Snatches the gold.

TRICE - What a devil do'st thou put up? Not my gold, I hope, Jack?

LOVEBY - By your favour, but I do; and 'twas won fairly: a sixieme, and fourteen by aces, by your own confession,--What a pox, we don't make childrens' play, I hope?

TRICE - Well, remember this, Jack; from this hour I forswear playing with you when I am alone; what, will you bate me nothing on't?

LOVEBY - Not a farthing, Justice; I'll be judged by you; if I had lost, you would have taken every piece on't: What I win, I win--and there's an end.

Enter Servant.

SERVANT - Sir, these people stay without, and will not be answered.

TRICE - Well, what's their business?

SERVANT -Nay, no great matter; only a fellow for getting a wench with child.

TRICE - No great matter, say'st thou? 'Faith, but it is. Is he a poor fellow, or a gentleman?

SERVANT - A very poor fellow, sir.

TRICE - Hang him, rogue; make his mittimus immediately; must such as he presume to get children?

LOVEBY - Well considered: A poor lousy rascal, to intrench upon the game of gentlemen! He might have passed his time at nine-pins, or shovel-board; that had been fit sport for such as he: Justice, have no mercy on him.

TRICE - No, by the sword of justice will I not.

LOVEBY - Swear'st thou, ungracious boy[A]? That's too much, on the other hand, for a gentleman. I swear not, I drink not, I curse not, I cheat not; they are unnecessary vices: I save so much out of those sins, and take it out in that one necessary vice of wenching.

[Footnote A: Henry IV. Part 1. Act ii. Scene 4.]

Enter LOVEBY'S Boy:

BOY - Sir, the parties are without, according to your order.

LOVEBY - 'Tis well; bring 'em in, boy.

Enter Lady Du LAKE, and two or three Whores.

Justice, I recommend this ancient gentlewoman, with these virtuous ladies, to thy patronage; for her part, she is a person of exemplary life and behaviour; of singular conduct to break through, and patience to bear the assaults of fortune: A general benefactress of mankind, and, in fine, a promoter of that great work of nature, love.

TRICE - Or, as the vulgar translation hath it, a very sufficient and singular good bawd: Is't not so, boy?

LOVEBY - Ay, boy: Now for such a pettifogging fellow as thy clerk to persecute this lady; pr'ythee think on't: Tis a grievance of the free-born subject.

LADY Du LAKE - To see the ingratitude of this generation! That I, that have spent my youth; set at nought my fortune; and, what is more dear to me, my honour, in the service of gentlemen; should now, in my old age, be left to want and beggary, as if I were the vilest and most unworthy creature upon God's earth! [Crying.

LOVEBY - Nay, good mother, do not take it so bitterly.

LADY Du LAKE - I confess, the unkindness of it troubles me.

LOVEBY - Thou shalt not want, so long as I live.--Look, here's five pieces of cordial gold, to comfort thy heart with: I won it, e'en now, off Mr Justice; and I dare say he thinks it well bestowed.

TRICE - My money's gone to very pious uses.

LADY Du LAKE - [Laying her hand on LOVEBY'S head.] Son Loveby, I knew thy father well; and thy grandfather before him. Fathers they were both to me; and I could weep for joy to see how thou tak'st after them. [Weeping again.] I wish it lay in my power too to gratify this worthy Justice in my vocation.

TRICE - 'Faith, I doubt I am past that noble sin.

LOVEBY - Pr'ythee, good magistrate, drink to her, and wipe sorrow from her eyes.

TRICE - Right reverend, my service to you in canary. [She drinks after him, and stays at half a glass.

LADY Du LAKE - 'Tis a great way to the bottom; but heaven is all-sufficient to give me strength for it. [Drinks it up.] Why, God's blessing on your heart, son Trice! I hope 'tis no offence to call you son?

hem!--hem!--Son Loveby, I think my son Trice and I are much of the same years: let me see, son, if nature be utterly extinct in you: Are you ticklish, son Trice? [Tickles him.

TRICE - Are you ticklish, Mother Du Lake?

[Tickles her sides. She falls off her chair; he falls off his to her; they roll one over the other.

LOVEBY - I would have all London now show me such another sight of kindness in old age. [They help each other up.] Come, a dance, a dance; call for your clerk, Justice; he shall make one, in sign of amity. Strike up, fidlers!

[They dance a round dance, and sing the tune.

Enter ISABELLA and CONSTANCE.

ISABELLA - Are you at that sport, i'faith? Have among you, blind harpers. [She falls into the dance.

[At the dance's ending, LOVEBY sees CONSTANCE.

TRICE - Is she come? A pox of all honest women at such a time!

LOVEBY - If she knows who these are, by this light, I am undone.

CONSTANCE - Oh, servant! I come to mind you of your promise. Come, produce my hundred pounds; the time's out I set you.

LOVEBY - Not till dark night, upon my reputation! I have not yet spoke with the gentleman in the black pantaloons; you know he seldom walks abroad by day-light. Dear madam, let me wait on you to your coach; and, if I bring it not within this hour, discard me utterly.

CONSTANCE - You must give me leave to salute the company. What are they?

LOVEBY - Persons of quality of my acquaintance; but I'll make your excuse to 'em.

CONSTANCE - Nay, if they are persons of quality, I shall be rude to part from 'em so abruptly.

LOVEBY - Why so?--the devil owed me a shame; and now he has paid me. I must present 'em, whate'er come on't. [Aside.]--This, madam, is my Lady Du Lake--the Lady Springwell--the Lady Hoyden.

[She and ISABELLA salute them.

ISABELLA - What a whiff was there came from my Lady Hoyden; and what a garlic breath my Lady Springwell had!

TRICE - Ha, ha, ha, ha!

LOVEBY - Do not betray me, Justice; if you do--[Aside.

ISABELLA - Oh, are you thereabouts, sir? then I smell a rat, i'faith; but I'll say nothing. [Aside.

CONSTANCE - Ladies, I am an humble servant to you all; and account it my happiness to have met with so good company at my cousin Trice's.

TRICE - Ha, ha, ha!

LADY Du LAKE - Are these two ladies of your acquaintance, son Loveby?

LOVEBY - Son, quoth a'! a pox of our relation! [Aside.

LADY Du LAKE - I shall be glad to be better known to your ladyships.

CONSTANCE - You too much honour your servants, madam.

ISABELLA - How Loveby fidges up and down! In what pain he is! well, if these be not they, they call whores, I'll be hanged, though I never saw one before. [Aside.

LOVEBY - Will your ladyship please to go, madam?

CONSTANCE - I must beg the favour of these ladies first, that I may know their lodgings, and wait on them.

LADY Du. LAKE - It will be our duty to pay our respects first to your ladyship.

CONSTANCE - I beg your ladyship's pardon, madam--

LADY Du LAKE - Your ladyship shall excuse us, madam--

ISABELLA - Trice. Ha, ha, ha!

LOVEBY - Ah, devil grin you! [Aside.

TRICE - I must go out, and laugh my belly-full.

[Exit TRICE.

CONSTANCE - But in earnest, madam, I must have no denial; I beseech your ladyship instruct me, where I may tender my devoirs.

LADY Du LAKE - Since your ladyship commands me, madam, I dare disobey no longer. My lodgings are in St Lucknor's Lane, at the Cat and Fiddle.

CONSTANCE - Whereabouts is that lane, servant?

LOVEBY - Faith, madam, I know not that part o'the town.--Lord, how I sweat for fear! [Aside.

CONSTANCE - And yours, madam, where, I beseech your ladyship?

2ND WHORE - In Dog and Bitch yard, an't please your ladyship.

3RD WHORE - And mine in Sodom, so like your ladyship.

CONSTANCE - How, Loveby! I did not think you would have used me thus?

LOVEBY - I beseech your ladyship, but hear my justification as I lead you.

CONSTANCE - By no means, sir; that were such a rudeness to leave persons of quality, to wait upon me: Unhand me, sir.

ISABELLA - Ha, ha, ha!--[Exeunt CONSTANCE, ISABELLA.

LOVEBY - I am ruined! for ever ruined. Plague, had you no places in the town to name, but Sodom, and Lucknor's Lane, for lodgings!

LADY Du LAKE - If any prejudice arise from it, upon my honour, son, 'twas by mistake, and not intended you: I thought she desired to have been admitted of the quality.

LOVEBY - I was curst, when I had first to do with you.

[Kicks them.

LADY Du LAKE - Well, I thank heaven, that has indued me with such patience.

[Exeunt all but LOVEBY and his Boy.

LOVEBY - I have made a fair hand on't to-day;--both lost my mistress, and hear no news from my friend below: The world frowns upon me, and the devil and my mistress have forsaken me: My godfathers and godmothers have promised well for me: Instead of renouncing them, they have renounced me.

BOY - Sir, I saw my Lady Constance smile as she went out: I am confident she's angry but from the teeth outwards: you might easily make fair weather with her, if you could get the money you promised her, but there's the devil--

LOVEBY - Where is he, boy? shew me him quickly.

BOY - Marry, God bless us! I mean, sir, there's the difficulty.

LOVEBY - Damned rogue, to put me in hope so--

Enter BIBBER at the other end.

LOVEBY - Uds so, look where Bibber is: Now I think on't, he offered me a bag of forty pounds, and the lease of his house yesterday: But that's his pocky humour; when I have money, and do not ask him, he will offer it; but when I ask him, he will not lend a farthing.--Turn this way, sirrah, and make as though we did not see him.

BIBBER - Our gentleman, I think, a-talking with his boy there.

LOVEBY - You understand me?--

BOY - I warrant you, sir.

LOVEBY - No news yet; what an unlucky rascal 'tis! if the rogue should hereafter be reduced to the raiment of his own shreds, I should not pity him.

BIBBER - How's this!

LOVEBY - Now is this rascal hunting after jests, to make himself the greatest to all that know him.

BIBBER - This must be me.

BOY - I can hear neither tale nor tidings of him: I have searched him in all his haunts; amongst his creditors; and in all companies where they are like to break the least jest. I have visited the coffee-houses for him; but among all the news there, I heard none of him.

BIBBER - Good, i' faith.

LOVEBY - Where's the warrant? I'll put in my own name, since I cannot find him.

BOY - Sir, I gave it a scrivener at next door, because I could not write, to fill up the blank place with Mr Bibber's name.

LOVEBY - What an unlucky vermin 'tis! now, for an hundred pound, could I have gratified him with a waiter's place at the custom-house, that had been worth to him an hundred pound a-year upon the nail.

BIBBER - Could you so, could you so, sir? give me your hand, and I thank you heartily, Mr Loveby.

LOVEBY - Art thou honest Will? faith, 'tis not worth thy thanks, till it be done: I wish I had the money for thee.

BIBBER - How much is't, sir?

LOVEBY - An hundred pounds would do it.

BIBBER - Let me see: forty, I have already by me; take that in part, sir;--and that, and the lease of my house, would over-do it.

LOVEBY - By all means thy lease, Will: ne'er scruple at that; hang a piece of parchment, and two bits of soft wax! thou shalt do't, thou shalt, boy.

BIBBER - Why, then I will, sir:--But stay, stay: now I think on't, Frances has one hundred and twenty pieces of old grandam-and-aunt gold left her, that she would never let me touch: if we could get that, Mr Loveby! but she'll never part with it.

LOVEBY - Tis but saying the place is for her; a waiting woman's place in the custom-house: Boy, go, and tell her on't immediately. [Exit Boy

BIBBER - Hold a little; she has been very desirous to get a place in court, that she might take place as the queen's servant.

LOVEBY - She shall have a dresser's place, if thou'lt keep counsel. The worst on't is, I have never a warrant ready.

BIBBER - 'Tis all one for that, sir; she can neither write nor read; 'tis but my telling her 'tis a warrant, and all's well. I can't but laugh to think how she'll be choused.

LOVEBY - And you too: [Aside.] Mum, she's here, Will.

Enter FRANCES.

FRANCES - A waiting-woman's place in the custom-house! there's news for me! thank you, kind Mr Loveby; you have been instrumental, I hear, of my preferment.

LOVEBY - No, 'tis a dresser's place at court, landlady.

FRANCES - O gemini! that's better news.

BIBBER - Aye, but you must make haste and fetch an hundred pieces: I can assure you five hundred are bidden for it: And the courtiers are such slippery youths, they are ever for the fairest chapman.

FRANCES - I'll fetch it presently;--oh how my heart quops now, as they say: I'll fetch it presently: Sweet Mr Loveby, if the business can be done, it shall be a good thing in your worship's way, I promise you: O the father! that it could be done: O sweet father! [Loveby plucks out a paper.

LOVEBY - Here, Mr Bibber, pray put in Madam Bibber's name into the warrant.

BIBBER - Madam Bibber! there's joy!--I must call you wife no more, 'tis Madam Bibber now.

FRANCES - Pray read it, Mr Bibber.

BIBBER - An order for the admission of the illustrious lady, Madam Bibber, into her majesty's service.

FRANCES - Pray give me the paper, I'll have nobody touch it but myself; I am sure my money pays for it, as they say. These are the finest words; Madam Bibber! pray, chicken, shew me where Madam is written, that I may kiss it all over. I shall make bold now to bear up to those flirting gentlewomen, that sweep it up and down with their long tails. I thought myself as good as they, when I was as I was; but now I am as I am.

LOVEBY - Good landlady, dispatch, and bring the money--

FRANCES - Truly, in the place of a dresser, I dare be bold to say, as they say, I shall give their majesties worships good content: I'll go fetch it.

[Exit FRANCES.

BIBBER - We must keep the poor soul in ignorance as long as we can, sir; for when she has once smoked it, I have no other way but to retreat into the body of my janizaries, my journey-men; and never come out into her presence more. Where will you be at nine o'clock, sir, that we may rejoice over our good fortune?

LOVEBY - Call me at my Lord Nonsuch's house, and I'll go with you.

BIBBER - We'll have the fiddles, and triumph, i'faith.

[Exit BIBBER.

LOVEBY - Lord, how eager this vermin was to cheat himself! Well, I'll after; I long to finger these Jacobus's: Perhaps they may make my peace again with my mistress.

[Exit LOVEBY.

SCENE II

Enter FAILER and NONSUCH. [CONSTANCE and ISABELLA listening.]

FAILER - I vow to gad, my lord, Sir Timorous is the most dejected person in the world, and full of regret for what is past. 'Twas his misfortune to be drawn in by such a person as Madam Isabella.

NONSUCH - Tis well his estate pleads for him; he should ne'er set foot more within my doors else.

FAILER - I'll be security for him for time to come: Leave it to me to get the licence: All I desire is, your daughter may be ready to-morrow morning.

NONSUCH - Well, let me alone with her.

[Exuent FAILER and NONSUCH.

ISABELLA - You heard the dreadful sound, to-morrow, cousin.

CONSTANCE - I would not throw myself away upon this fool, if I could help it.

ISABELLA - Better marry a tertian ague than a fool, that's certain; there's one good day and night in that.

CONSTANCE - And yet thou art mad for him thyself.

ISABELLA - Nay, the fool is a handsome fool, that's somewhat; but 'tis not that; 'tis a kind of fancy I have taken to a glass coach, and six Flanders mares; rich liveries, and a good fortune.

CONSTANCE - Pr'ythee do not mind me of 'em; for though I want 'em not, yet I find all women are caught with gaieties: One grain more would turn the balance on his side; I am so vexed at the wild courses of this Loveby.

ISABELLA - Vexed? why vexed? the worst you can say of him is, he loves women: And such make the kindest husbands, I'm told. If you had a sum of money to put out, you would not look so much whether the man were an honest man, (for the law would make him that) as if he were a good sufficient pay-master.

Enter SETSTONE.

CONSTANCE - As I live, thou art a mad girl.

SETSTONE - She must be used as mad folks are then; had into the dark and cured.

CONSTANCE - But all this is no comfort to the word, to-morrow.

ISABELLA - Well, what say you, if I put you to-night into the arms of Loveby?

CONSTANCE - My condition's desperate, and past thy physic.

ISABELLA - When physic's past, what remains but to send for the divine? here's little Nicodemus, your father's chaplain: I have spoke with him already; for a brace of angels he shall make all sure betwixt you without a license; aye, and prove ten at night a more canonical hour than ten i'the morning.

CONSTANCE - I see not which way thou can'st perform it; but if thou do'st, I have many admirations in store for thee. [Whispers.

ISABELLA - Step in, and get a cushion underneath your apron.

CONSTANCE - O, I must be with child, it seems!

ISABELLA - And Loveby shall bring you to bed to-night, if the devil be not in the dice: away, make haste; [Exit CONSTANCE.] Setstone, be not you far off: I shall have need of you too: I hear my uncle coming--Methinks I long to be revenged of this wicked elder, for hindering of my marriage to-day: Hark you, Setstone-- [Whispers;

SETSTONE - Tis impossible, madam; 'twill never take.

ISABELLA - I warrant you; do not I know him? he has not brains enough, if they were buttered, to feed a blackbird--Nay, no replies--out of what I have said, you may instruct my cousin too.

[Exit SETSTONE.

Enter NONSUCH.

ISABELLA - Oh, are you there, sir? Faith, it was kindly done of you to hinder me of a good husband this afternoon: And but for one thing, I would resolve to leave your house.

NONSUCH - I'm glad there's any thing will stay thee.

ISABELLA - If I stay, 'tis for love of my cousin Constance, not of you: I should be loth to leave her in this sad condition.

NONSUCH - What condition?

ISABELLA - Nay, I know not; she has not worn her busk this fortnight. I think she's grown fat o'the sudden.

NONSUCH - O devil, devil! what a fright I'm in!

ISABELLA - She has qualms too every morning: ravens mightily for green fruit; and swoons at the sight of hot meat.

NONSUCH - She's with child: I am undone! I am undone!

ISABELLA - I understand nothing of such matters: She's but in the next room; best call her, and examine her about it.

NONSUCH - Why Constance, Constance!

Enter CONSTANCE, as with child.

ISABELLA - Now for a broad-side; turn your prow to him, cousin.

[To her.

NONSUCH - Now, gentlewoman! is this possible?

CONSTANCE - I do not reach your meaning, sir.

NONSUCH - Where have you been of late?

CONSTANCE - I seldom stir without you, sir: These walls most commonly confine me.

NONSUCH - These walls can get no children; nor these hangings; though there be men wrought in 'em.

ISABELLA - Yet, by your favour, nuncle, children may be wrought behind the hangings.

NONSUCH - O Constance, Constance! How have my grey hairs deserved this of thee? Who got that belly there?

CONSTANCE - You, I hope, sir.

NONSUCH - Tell me the truth, for I will know it; come, the story.

CONSTANCE - The story's quickly told, sir; I am with child.

NONSUCH - And who is the father?

CONSTANCE - I do not know, sir.

NONSUCH - Not know! went there so many to't?

CONSTANCE - So far from that, that there were none at all, to my best knowledge, sir.

NONSUCH - Was't got by miracle? Who was the father?

CONSTANCE - Who got your money, sir, that you have lost?

NONSUCH - Nay, Heaven knows who got that.

CONSTANCE - And, Heaven knows who got this: for, on my conscience, he, that had your money, was the father on't.

NONSUCH - The devil it was as soon.

CONSTANCE - That's all I fear, sir.

ISABELLA - 'Tis strange;--and yet 'twere hard, sir, to suspect my cousin's virtue, since we know the house is haunted.

NONSUCH - 'Tis true, that nothing can be laid, though under lock and key, but it miscarries.

ISABELLA - 'Tis not to be believed, what these villainous spirits can do: they go invisible.

CONSTANCE - First, they stole away my prayer-book; and, a little after that, a small treatise I had against temptation; and when they were gone, you know, sir--

ISABELLA - If there be such doings, pray heaven we are not all with child. 'Tis certain, that none live within these walls, but they have power of: I have reared Toby, the coachman, any time this fortnight.

NONSUCH - Out, impudence! A man with child! why 'tis unnatural.

ISABELLA - Ay, so is he that got it.

NONSUCH - Thou art not in earnest?

ISABELLA - I would I were not:--Hark! I hear him groan hither. Come in, poor Toby.

Enter TOBY, the coachman, with an urinal.

NONSUCH - How now! what have you there, sirrah?

TOBY - An't please your worship, 'tis my water. I had a spice o'the new disease here i'the house; and so carried it to master doctor.

NONSUCH - Well; and what did he say to you?

TOBY - He told me very sad news, an' please you: I am somewhat bashful to speak on't.

ISABELLA - Out with it, man.

TOBY - Why, truly, he told me, the party that owned the water was with child.

ISABELLA - I told you so, uncle.

NONSUCH - To my best remembrance, I never heard of such a thing before.

TOBY - I never stretch out myself to snap my whip, but it goes to the heart of me.

ISABELLA - Alas, poor Toby!

NONSUCH - Begone, and put off your livery, sirrah!--You shall not stay a minute in my service.

TOBY - I beseech your good worship, be good to me; 'twas the first fault I ever committed in this kind. I have three poor children by my wife; and if you leave me to the wide world, with a new charge upon myself--

NONSUCH - Begone! I will not hear a word.

TOBY - If I must go, I'll not go alone: Ambrose Tinis, the cook, is as bad as I am.

NONSUCH - I think you'll make me mad. Call the rascal hither! I must account with him on another score, now I think on't.

Enter AMBROSE TINIS.

NONSUCH - Sirrah, what made you send a pheasant with one wing to the table yesterday?

AMBROSE TINIS - I beseech your worship to pardon me; I longed for't.

ISABELLA - I feared as much.

AMBROSE TINIS - And I beseech your worship let me have a boy, to help me in the kitchen; for I find myself unable to go through with the work. Besides, the doctor has warned me of stooping to the fire, for fear of a mischance.

NONSUCH - Why, are you with child, sirrah?

AMBROSE TINIS - So he tells me; but, if I were put to my oath, I know not that ever I deserved for't.

NONSUCH - Still worse and worse. And here comes Setstone groaning.

Enter SETSTONE.

SETSTONE - O, sir! I have been so troubled with swooning fits; and have so longed for cherries!

NONSUCH - He's poopt too.

ISABELLA - Well, this is not the worst yet: I suspect something more than I will speak of.

NONSUCH - What dost thou suspect, ha!

ISABELLA - Is not your lordship with child, too?

NONSUCH - Who, I with child! marry, heaven forbid! What dost thou see by me, to ground it on?

ISABELLA - You're very round of late;--that's all, sir.

NONSUCH - Round! that's only fat, I hope. I have had a very good stomach of late, I'm sure.

ISABELLA - Alas, and well you may;--You eat for two, sir.

NONSUCH - Setstone, look upon me, and tell me true: Do you observe any alteration in me?

SETSTONE - I would not dishearten your ladyship--your lordship, I would say--but I have observed, of late, your colour goes and comes extremely. Methinks your lordship looks very sharp, and bleak i'the face, and mighty puffed i'the body.

NONSUCH - O, the devil! Wretched men, that we are all! Nothing grieves me, but that, in my old age, when others are past child-bearing, I should come to be a disgrace to my family.

CONSTANCE - How do you, sir? Your eyes look wondrous dim. Is not there a mist before 'em?

ISABELLA - Do you not feel a kicking in your belly--When do you look, uncle?

NONSUCH - Uh, uh!--Methinks, I am very sick o'the sudden.

ISABELLA - What store of old shirts have you against the good time? Shall I give you a shift, uncle?

NONSUCH - Here's like to be a fine charge towards! We shall all be brought to-bed together! Well, if I be with devil, I will have such gossips: an usurer, and a scrivener, shall be godfathers.

ISABELLA - I'll help you, uncle; and Sawney's two grannies shall be godmothers. The child shall be christened by the directory; and the gossips' gifts shall be the gude Scotch kivenant.

CONSTANCE - Set. Non. Tob. Amb. Uh! uh! uh!

ISABELLA - What rare music's here!

NONSUCH - Whene'er it comes from me, 'twill kill me; that's certain.

SETSTONE - Best take a vomit.

ISABELLA - An't come upward, the horns will choke him.

NONSUCH - Mass! and so they will.

ISABELLA - Your only way, is to make sure o'the man-midwife.

NONSUCH - But my child's dishonour troubles me the most. If I could but see her well married, before I underwent the labour and peril of child-bearing!--What would you advise, niece?

ISABELLA - That which I am very loth to do. Send for honest Jack Loveby, and let him know the truth on't: He's a fellow without a fortune, and will be glad to leap at the occasion.

NONSUCH - But why Loveby, of all the world? 'Tis but staying 'till to-morrow, and then Sir Timorous will marry her.

CONSTANCE - Uh!--I swell so fast, I cannot hide it 'till to-morrow.

ISABELLA - Why, there's it now!

NONSUCH - I'll send for the old alderman, Getwell, immediately: He'll father the devil's bastard, I warrant you.

ISABELLA - Fie, uncle! my cousin's somewhat too good yet for an alderman. If it were her third child, she might hearken to you.

NONSUCH - Well, since it must be so, Setstone, go you to Loveby; make my excuse to him for the arrest, and let him know, what fortune may attend him.

ISABELLA - Mr Setstone, pray acquaint him with my cousin's affection to him; and prepare him to father the cushion underneath her petticoat.

[Aside to SETSTONE. Exit.]

SETSTONE - I'll bring him immediately.

ISABELLA - When he comes, uncle, pray cover your great belly with your hat, that he may not see it.

NONSUCH - It goes against my heart to marry her to this Loveby; but, what must be, must be.

Enter LOVEBY.

CONSTANCE - O, Mr Loveby! The welcomest man alive! You met Setstone, I hope, that you came so opportunely?

LOVEBY - No, faith, madam; I came of my own accord.

ISABELLA - 'Tis unlucky; he's not prepared.

LOVEBY - Look you, madam, I have brought the hundred pounds; the devil was as punctual as three o' clock at a playhouse. Here; 'tis right, I warrant it, without telling: I took it upon his word.

[Gives it.

CONSTANCE - Your kindness shall be requited, servant: But I sent for you upon another business. Pray, cousin, tell it him, for I am ashamed to do't.

LOVEBY - Ha! 'tis not that great belly, I hope. Is't come to that?

ISABELLA - Hark you, Mr Loveby; a word with you.

LOVEBY - A word with you, madam: Whither is your cousin bound?

ISABELLA - Bound, sir?

LOVEBY - Ay, bound: Look you, she's under sail, with a lusty fore-wind.

NONSUCH - I sent for you, sir; but, to be plain with you, 'twas more out of necessity than love.

LOVEBY - I wonder, my lord, at your invincible ill-nature. You forget the arrest, that I passed by: But this it is to be civil to unthankful persons; 'tis feeding an ill-natured dog, that snarls while he takes victuals from your hand.

NONSUCH - All friends! all friends! No ripping up old stories; you shall have my daughter.

LOVEBY - Faith, I see your lordship would let lodgings ready furnished; but I am for an empty tenement.

NONSUCH - I had almost forgot my own great belly. If he should discover that too! [Claps his hat before it.

ISABELLA - [To Lov.] You will not hear me, sir. 'Tis all roguery, as I live.

LOVEBY - Flat roguery, I'll swear! If I had been father on't, nay, if I had but laid my breeches upon the bed, I would have married her: But I see we are not ordained for one another.

[Is going.

NONSUCH - I beseech you, sir.

LOVEBY - Pray cover, my lord.

ISABELLA - He does his great belly, methinks.

NONSUCH - I'll make it up in money to you.

LOVEBY - That cannot tempt me. I have a friend, that shall be nameless, that will not see me want; and so, your servant.

[Exit LOVEBY.

ISABELLA - I'll after, and bring him back.

NONSUCH - You shall not stir after him;--Does he scorn my daughter?

ISABELLA - Lord, how fretful you are! This breeding makes you so peevish, uncle.

NONSUCH - 'Tis no matter, she shall straight be married to Sir Timorous.

CONSTANCE - I am ruined, cousin.

[Aside.

ISABELLA - I warrant you.--My lord, I wish her well married to Sir Timorous; but Loveby will certainly infect him with the news of her great belly.

NONSUCH - I'll dispatch it, ere he can speak with him.

ISABELLA - Whene'er he comes, he'll see what a bona roba she is grown.

NONSUCH - Therefore, it shall be done i'the evening.

ISABELLA - It shall, my lord.

CONSTANCE - Shall it?

[Aside.

ISABELLA - Let me alone, cousin.--And to this effect she shall write to him, that, to conform to your will, and his modesty, she desires him to come hither alone this evening.

NONSUCH - Excellent wench!--I'll get my chaplain ready.

[Exit NONSUCH.

CONSTANCE - How can you hope to deceive my father?

ISABELLA - If I don't, I have hard luck.

CONSTANCE - You go so strange a way about, your bowl must be well bias'd to come in.

ISABELLA - So plain a ground, there's not the least rub in't. I'll meet Sir Timorous in the dark; and, in your room, marry him.

CONSTANCE - You'll be sure to provide for one.

ISABELLA - You mistake me, cousin:--Oh! here's Setstone again.

Enter SETSTONE.

Mr Jeweller, you must again into your devil's shape, and speak with Loveby. But pray be careful not to be discovered.

SETSTONE - I warrant you, madam. I have cozened wiser men than he in my own shape; and, if I cannot continue it in a worse, let the devil, I make bold with, e'en make as bold with me.

ISABELLA - You must guide him, by back ways, to my uncle's house, and so to my cousin's chamber, that he may not know where he is when he comes there. The rest I'll tell you as we go along.

[Exuent.

SCENE III

Enter TIMOROUS; after him BURR and FAILER.

TIMOROUS - Here, here, read this note; there's news for us.

FAILER - Let me see't. [Reads.

Sir Timorous, Be at the garden-door at nine this evening; there I'll receive you with my daughter. To gratify your modesty I designed this way, after I had better considered on it: and pray leave your caterpillars, Burr and Failer, behind you. Yours, Nonsuch.

There is some trick in this, whate'er it be. But this word, caterpillars--You see, Burr, Sir Timorous is like to be lured from us. [Aside.

BURR - Is there no prevention? [Aside.

FAILER - One way there is.--Sir Timorous, pray walk a turn, while Burr and I confer a little upon this matter.--Look you, Burr, there is but one remedy in nature, I vow to gad; that is, for you to have a new Sir Timorous, exceeding this person in bounty to you. Observe, then; in Sir Timorous' place will I go, and, egad, I'll marry my lady Constance; and then, from the bowels of friendship, bless thee with a thousand pounds, besides lodging and diet for thy life, boy.

BURR - Umph, very well thought on.--No, sir! you shall trust to my bounty; I'll go in his place. Murmur or repine, speak the least word, or give thy lips the least motion, and I'll beat thee till thou art not in condition to go.

FAILER - I vow to gad, this is extreme injustice.--Was it not my invention?

BURR - Why, dost thou think thou art worthy to make use of thy own invention?--Speak another word, d'ye see!--Come, help me quickly to strip Sir Timorous; his coat may conduce to the deceit.-- Sir Timorous, by your leave. [Fatts on him.

TIMOROUS - O, Lord! what's the matter?--Murder? murder!

BURR - D'ye open? I have something in my pocket that will serve for a gag, now I think on't.

[Gags, and binds him.

So, lie there, knight. Come, sir, and help to make me Sir Timorous; and, when I am married, remember to increase your manners with my fortune.--Yet we'll always drink together. [Exuent.

ACT V

SCENE I

Enter CONSTANCE, ISABELLA, and NONSUCH.

CONSTANCE - This is just the knight's hour; and lovers seldom come after their time.

NONSUCH - Good night, daughter; I'll to bed, and give you joy to-morrow morning. [Exit.

ISABELLA - I'm glad he's gone: What, your train takes?

CONSTANCE - Yes, yes; Loveby will come: Setstone has been with him in disguise; and promised him golden mountains, if he will not be wanting to his own fortune.

ISABELLA - Is your habit provided too?

CONSTANCE - All is ready.

ISABELLA - Away then; for this is the place where we must part like knights errant, that take several paths to their adventures.

CONSTANCE - 'Tis time, for I hear somebody come along the alley; without question 'tis Timorous. Farewell; the chaplain stays for me in the chamber.

ISABELLA - And I'll post after you to matrimony; I have laid a fresh parson at the next stage, that shall carry me tantivy.

[Exit CONSTANCE.

Enter BURR with TIMOROUS'S coat on.

BURR - My lady Constance!

ISABELLA - The same: Sir Timorous?

BURR - The same.

ISABELLA - Sir Timorous takes me for my cousin.

[Aside.

BURR - My lady Constance mistakes me for the knight.

[Aside.

ISABELLA - Here, sir; through the dark walk: 'tis but a little way about--He's my own beyond redemption--

[Aside.

BURR - The Indies are mine; and a handsome lady into the bargain.

[Exeunt.

Enter FAILER, dogging them, as they go off.

FAILER - He shall be hanged, ere he shall get her. Thus far I have dogged them, and this way I am sure they must pass, ere they come to the house. The rogue had got the old dog-trick of a statesman; to fish things out of wiser heads than his own, and never so much as to take notice of him that gave the counsel--

Enter ISABELLA and BURR again.

Now, if I can but give her the hint without his knowledge!--Madam--my lady Constance!

ISABELLA - What voice is that?

FAILER - A word in private, or you are undone--Pray step aside.

BURR - Where are you, madam?

ISABELLA - Immediately, Sir Timorous.

FAILER - You are mistaken, madam; 'tis not Sir Timorous, but Burr in his clothes; he has stripped the knight, gagged him, and locked him up.

ISABELLA - Failer?

FAILER - The same. I could not but prevent your unhappiness, though I hazard my person in the discovery, I vow to gad, madam.

BURR - Who's that talks to you, my lady Constance?

ISABELLA - A maid of my acquaintance, that's come to take her leave of me before I marry; the poor soul does so pity me.

BURR - How will that maid lie, thinking of you and me to-night!

ISABELLA - Has he the key about him? [To FAILER.

FAILER - I think so, madam.

ISABELLA - Could not you possibly pick his pocket, and give me the key? then let me alone to release Sir Timorous; and you shall be witness of the wedding.

FAILER - Egad, you want your cousin Isabella's wit to bring that to pass, madam.

ISABELLA - I warrant you, my own wit will serve to fool Burr--and you too, or I am much deceived. [Aside.

FAILER - I am a little apprehensive of the rascal's fingers, since I felt them last; and yet my fear has not power to resist the sweet temptation of revenge; I vow to gad I'll try, madam.

ISABELLA - Never fear; let me alone to keep him busy.

BURR - Come, madam, and let me take off these tasteless kisses the maid gave you; may we not join lips before we are married?

ISABELLA - No; fie, Sir Timorous.

[They struggle a little, and in that time FAILER picks his pocket of the key.

FAILER - I have it--here it is--now, shift for yourself, as I'll do; I'll wait you in the alley.

[Exit.

ISABELLA - Sir Timorous, pray go into my chamber, and make no noise till I return; I'll but fetch the little man of God, and follow you in a twinkling.

BURR - There's no light, I hope?

ISABELLA - Not a spark.

BURR - For to light me to the mark--

[Exit.

ISABELLA - What a scowering have I 'scaped to-night! Fortune, 'tis thou hast been ingenious for me! Allons, Isabella! Courage! now to deliver my knight from the enchanted castle.

[Exit.

Enter LOVEBY, led by SETSTONE, antickly habited; with a torch in one hand, and a wand in the other.

LOVEBY - What art thou, that hast led me this long hour through lanes and alleys, and blind passages?

SETSTONE - I am thy genius; and conduct thee to wealth, fame, and honour; what thou comest to do, do boldly; fear not; with this rod I charm thee; and neither elf nor goblin now can harm thee.

LOVEBY - Well, march on; if thou art my genius, thou art bound to be answerable for me; I'll have thee hanged, if I miscarry.

SETSTONE - Fear not, my son.

LOVEBY - Fear not, quotha! then, pr'ythee, put on a more familiar shape:--one of us two stinks extremely: Pr'ythee, do not come so near me; I do not love to have my face bleached like a tiffany with thy brimstone.

SETSTONE - Fear not, but follow me.

LOVEBY - 'Faith, I have no great mind to't; I am somewhat godly at present; but stay a month longer, and I'll be proud, and fitter for thee. In the mean time, pr'ythee, stay thy stomach with some Dutchman; an Hollander, with butter, will fry rarely in hell.

SETSTONE - Mortal, 'tis now too late for a retreat; go on, and live; step back, and thou art mine.

LOVEBY - So I am, however, first or last; but for once I'll trust thee. [Exeunt.

SCENE II

The scene opens, and discovers CONSTANCE, and a Parson by her; she habited like Fortune.

Enter again.

SETSTONE - Take here the mighty queen of good and ill, Fortune; first marry, then enjoy thy fill Of lawful pleasures; but depart ere morn; Slip from her bed, or else thou shalt be torn Piecemeal by fiends; thy blood caroused in bowls, And thy four quarters blown to the top of Paul's.

LOVEBY - By your favour, I'll never venture. Is marrying the business? I'll none, I thank you.

[Here CONSTANCE whispers TO SETSTONE.

SETSTONE - Fortune will turn her back if twice denied.

LOVEBY - Why, she may turn her girdle too on t'other side[A]. This is the devil; I will not venture on her.

[Footnote A: A usual expression of indifference for a man's displeasure.]

SETSTONE - Fear not; she swears thou shalt receive no harm.

LOVEBY - Ay, if a man durst trust her; but the devil is got into such an ill name of lying--

SETSTONE - Whene'er you are not pleased, it shall be lawful to sue out your divorce.

LOVEBY - Ay, but where shall I get a lawyer? there you are aforehand with me; you have retained most of them already. For the favours I have received, I am very much her servant; but, in the way of matrimony, Mr Parson there can tell you 'tis an ordinance, and must not be entered into without mature deliberation; besides, marriages, you know, are made in heaven; and that I am sure this was not.

SETSTONE - She bids you then, at least, restore that gold, which she, too lavishly, poured out on you, unthankful man.

LOVEBY - Faith, I have it not at present; 'tis all gone, as I am a sinner; but, 'tis gone wickedly; all spent in the devil her father's service.

SETSTONE - Where is the grateful sense of all your favours? Come, fiends, with flesh-hooks, tear the wretch in pieces, And bear his soul upon your leather wings, Below the fountain of the dark abyss.

LOVEBY - What, are you a-conjuring? If you are good at that sport, I can conjure as well as you-- [Draws his sword.

CONSTANCE - Hold; for Heaven's sake, hold! I am no spirit; touch but my hand; ghosts have no flesh and blood. [Discovering.

LOVEBY - My lady Constance! I began to suspect it might be a trick, but never could imagine you the author. It seems you are desirous I should father this hans en kelder here?

CONSTANCE - I know not how, without a blush, to tell you, it was a cheat I practised for your love.

SETSTONE - A mere tympany, sir, raised by a cushion; you see 'tis gone already.

CONSTANCE - Setstone was sent to have acquainted you; but, by the way, unfortunately missed you.

LOVEBY - Twas you, then, that supplied me all this while with money? pretty familiar, I hope to make thee amends ere I sleep to-night. Come, parson, pr'ythee make haste and join us. I long to be out of her debt, poor rogue.

[The parson takes them to the side of the stage; they turn their backs to the audience, while he mumbles to them.

SETSTONE - I'll be the clerk; Amen--give you joy, Mr Bridegroom, and Mrs Bride.

CONSTANCE - Thanks, honest Setstone.

[BIBBER, FRANCES, and music without--they play.

Music: God give your worship a good even, Mr Loveby.

CONSTANCE - Hark! what noise is that! Is this music of your providing, Setstone?

SETSTONE - Alas, madam, I know nothing of it.

LOVEBY - We are betrayed to your father; but the best on't is, he comes too late to hinder us--fear not, madam, I'll bear you through them all.

[As they rush out, BIBBER, FRANCES, and Music are entering in; BIBBER and FRANCES are beaten down. Exeunt LOVEBY; CONSTANCE, SETSTONE, and Parson.

ALL CRY OUT - Oh the devil! the devil! the devil!

BIBBER - Lord bless us, where are you, Frances!

FRANCES - Here, William! this is a judgment, as they say, upon you, William, for trusting wits, and calling gentlemen to the tavern, William.

BIBBER - No; 'twas a judgment upon you, for desiring preferment at court, Frances. Let's call up the watch, and Justice Trice, to have the house searched.

FRANCES - Ay, ay; there's more devils there, I warrant you. [Exeunt.

Enter LOVEBY, CONSTANCE, and SETSTONE again.

LOVEBY - It was certainly Will Bibber and his wife, with music; for, now I remember myself, I 'pointed him this hour at your father's house: but we frighted them worse than they frighted us.

CONSTANCE - Our parson ran away too, when they cried out the devil!

LOVEBY - He was the wiser; for if the devil had come indeed, he has preached so long against him, it would have gone hard with him.

SETSTONE - Indeed, I have always observed parsons to be more fearful of the devil than other people.

LOVEBY - Oh, the devil's the spirit, and the parson's the flesh; and betwixt those two there must be a war; yet, to do them both right, I think in my conscience they quarrel only like lawyers for their fees, and meet good friends in private, to laugh at their clients.

CONSTANCE - I saw him run in at my cousin Isabella's chamber door, which was wide open; I believe she's returned: We'll fetch a light from the gallery, and give her joy.

LOVEBY - Why, is she married, madam?

CONSTANCE - I'll tell you as we go. [Exeunt.

SCENE III

BURR and the PARSON enter, meeting in the dark.

BURR - My lady Constance, are you come again? That's well; I have waited sufficiently for you in the dark.

PARSON - Help, help, help, good Christian people! the devil, the devil's here.

BURR - 'Tis I, madam; what do you mean?

PARSON - Avoid, Satan! avoid, avoid.

BURR - What have I here, the hairy woman?

Enter LOVEBY, and CONSTANCE with the light.

Ha! yonder's my lady Constance! who have I got? a stone priest, by this good light. How's this, Loveby too!

LOVEBY - Burr a-beating my reverend clergy? What makes you here at this unseasonable hour? I'll know your business. [Draws.

BURR - Will you, sir? [They fight.

CONSTANCE - Set.

PARSON - Help, murder, murder!

Enter, at one door, TRICE drunk, with the Watch; BIBBER and FRANCES following; at the other, NONSUCH and Servants, and FAILER.

NONSUCH - Murder, murder! beat down their weapons. Will you murder Sir Timorous, Mr Loveby?-- [They disarm both.] Sir Timorous?--ha, Burr! Thieves, thieves!--sit down, good Mr Justice, and take their examinations. Now I shall know how my money went.

TRICE - They shall have justice, I warrant them. [Goes to sit, and misses the chair.

BIBBER - The justice is almost dead drunk, my lord.

FRANCES - But an't please your worship, my lord, this is not the worst sight that we have seen here to-night in your worship's house; we met three or four hugeous ugly devils, with eyes like saucers, that threw down my husband, that threw down me, that made my heart so panck ever since, as they say!

NONSUCH - The devil again in my house?

LOVEBY - Nay, here he was, that's certain; he brought me hither, I know not how myself, and married me; Mr Setstone there can justify it: But the best is, I have a charm about me, that will lay him yet ere midnight.

FAILER - And I vow to gad, my lord, I know as little how I came hither as any man.

BURR - Nor I.

TRICE - Nor I.

LOVEBY - No, I dare swear do'st thou not, Mr Justice.

TRICE - But I wonder how the devil durst come into our ward, when he knows I have been at the duties of--my family--this evening.

Enter one of the WATCH, with TIMOROUS and ISABELLA.

WATCH -An please your worship, I met this couple in the street late, and so, seeing them to be a man and woman, I brought them along with me, upon suspicion of felony together.

FRANCES - This is the proud minx, that sought shelter in my house this afternoon, Mr Justice.

FAILER - Sir Timorous and Madam Isabella! I vow to gad, we are undone, Burr.--

ISABELLA - Do not you know me, Mr Justice?

LOVEBY - Justice is blind, he knows nobody.

ISABELLA - My name is Isabella.

FRANCES - No, thy name is Jezebella; I warrant you, there's none but rogues and papists would be abroad at this time of night.

BIBBER - Hold, Frances.

TRICE - She's drunk, I warrant her, as any beast. I wonder, woman, you do not consider what a crying sin drunkenness is: Whom do you learn it from in our parish? I am sure you never see me worse.

ISABELLA - Burr and Failer, acknowledge yourselves a couple of recreant knights: Sir Timorous is mine: I have won him in fair field from you.

CONSTANCE - Give you joy, cousin, give you joy!

LOVEBY - Married!

ISABELLA - And in Diana's grove, boy.

LOVEBY - Why, 'tis fine, by Heaven; 'tis wondrous fine; as the poet goes on sweetly.

TIMOROUS - I am sure they had gagged me, and bound me, and stripped me almost stark naked, and locked me up as fast as a butterfly, 'till she came and made me a man again; and therefore I have reason to love her the longest day I have to live.

ISABELLA - Ay, and the longest night too, or you are to blame. And you have one argument I love you, if the proverb be true, for I took you almost in your bare shirt.

BURR - So much for us, Failer!

CONSTANCE - Well, my lord, it had as good out at first as at last: I must beg your lordship's blessing for this gentleman and myself. [Both kneel.

NONSUCH - Why, you are not married to him, I hope! he's married to the devil.

LOVEBY - 'Twas a white devil of your lordship's getting, then; Mr Setstone and the reverend here can witness it.

SETSTONE & PARSON - We must speak truth, my lord.

NONSUCH - Would I had another child for your sake! you should ne'er see a penny of my money.

LOVEBY - Thank you, my lord; but methinks 'tis much better as it is.

ISABELLA - Come, nuncle, 'tis in vain to hold out, now 'tis past remedy: 'Tis like the last act of a play, when people must marry; and if fathers will not consent then, they should throw oranges at them from the galleries. Why should you stand off, to keep us from a dance?

NONSUCH - But there's one thing still that troubles me; that's her great belly, and my own too.

CONSTANCE - Nay, for mine, my lord, 'tis vanished already; 'twas but a trick to catch the old one.

LOVEBY - But I'll do my best; she shall not be long without another.

ISABELLA - But as for your great belly, nuncle, I know no way to rid you on't, but by taking out your guts.

LOVEBY - 'Tis such a pretty smart rascal, 'tis well I am pleased with my own choice: but I could have got such Hectors, and poets, and gamesters, out of thee!--

CONSTANCE - No, no; two wits could never have lived well together; want would have so sharpened you upon one another.

ISABELLA - A wit should naturally be joined to a fortune; by the same reason your vintners feed their hungry wines.

CONSTANCE - And if Sir Timorous and I had married, we two fortunes must have built hospitals with our money; we could never have spent it else.

LOVEBY - Or what think you of paying courtiers' debts with it?

ISABELLA - Well, to shew I am in charity with my enemies, I'll make a motion: While we are in town, let us hire a large house, and live together: Burr and Failer--

FAILER - Shall be utterly discarded; I knew 'twould come to that, I vow to gad.

ISABELLA - Shall be our guests.

[BURR and FAILER throw up their caps, and cry, Vive Madam ISABELLA!

LOVEBY - And Bibber shall make our wedding clothes without trusting.

BIBBER - No, henceforward I'll trust none but landed men, and such as have houses and apple-trees in the country, now I have got a place in the custom-house.

FRANCES - Nothing vexes me, but that this flirting gentlewoman should go before me; but I'll to the herald's office, and see whether the queen's majesty's dresser, should not take place of any knight's wife in Christendom.

BIBBER - Now all will out--no more, good Frances.

FRANCES - I will speak, that I will, so I will: What! shall I be a dresser to the queen's majesty, and nobody must know on't? I'll send Mr Church-warden word on't; and, gentlemen, when you come to St Bride's church (if ever you come to church, gentlemen), you shall see me in the pew that's next the pulpit; thank Mr Loveby's worship for it.

LOVEBY - Spare your thanks, good landlady; for the truth is, they came too late, the place is gone; and so is yours, Will; but you shall have two hundred pounds for one, if that will satisfy you.

FRANCES - This is bitter news, as they say.

LOVEBY - Cheer up thy wife, Will. Where are the fiddles? A dance should do it.

BIBBER - I'll run and call them.

ISABELLA - I have found out that, will comfort her: Henceforward I christen her by the name of Madam Bibber.

All: A Madam Bibber, a Madam Bibber!

FRANCES - Why, I thank you, sweet gentlemen and ladies; this is a cordial to my drooping spirits: I confess I was a little eclipsed; but I'll cheer up with abundance of love, as they say. Strike up, fiddles.

LOVEBY - That's a good wench.

DANCE.

TRICE - This music and a little nod has recovered me. I'll in, and provide for the sack posset.

NONSUCH - To bed, to bed; 'tis late. Son Loveby, get me a boy to-night, and I'll settle three thousand a-year upon him the first day he calls me grandsire.

LOVEBY - I'll do my best, To make the bargain sure before I sleep. Where love and money strike, the blow goes deep.

[Exeunt omnes.

EPILOGUE, WHEN IT WAS FIRST ACTED

The Wild Gallant has quite played out his game;
He's married now, and that will make him tame;
Or if you think marriage will not reclaim him,
The critics swear they'll damn him, but they'll tame him.
Yet, though our poet's threatened most by these,
They are the only people he can please:
For he, to humour them, has shown to-day,
That which they only like, a wretched play:
But though his play be ill, here have been shown
The greatest wits, and beauties of the town;
And his occasion having brought you here,
You are too grateful to become severe.
There is not any person here so mean,
But he may freely judge each act and scene:
But if you bid him chuse his judges, then,
He boldly names true English gentlemen:
For he ne'er thought a handsome garb or dress
So great a crime, to make their judgment less:
And with these gallants he these ladies joins,
To judge that language, their converse refines.
But if their censures should condemn his play,
Far from disputing, he does only pray
He may Leander's destiny obtain:
Now spare him, drown him when he comes again.

EPILOGUE, WHEN REVIVED

Of all dramatic writing, comic wit,
As 'tis the best, so 'tis most, hard to hit.
For it lies all in level to the eye,
Where all may judge, and each defect may spy.
Humour is that, which every day we meet,
And therefore known as every public street;
In which, if e'er the poet go astray,

You all can point, 'twas there he lost his way.
But, what's so common, to make pleasant too,
Is more than any wit can always do.
For 'tis like Turks, with hen and rice to treat;
To make regalios out of common meat.
But, in your diet, you grow savages:
Nothing but human flesh your taste can please;
And, as their feasts with slaughtered slaves began,
So you, at each new play, must have a man.
Hither you come, as to see prizes fought;
If no blood's drawn, you cry, the prize is naught.
But fools grow wary now; and, when they see
A poet eyeing round the company,
Straight each-man for himself begins to doubt;
They shrink like seamen when a press comes out.
Few of them will be found for public use,
Except you charge an oaf upon each house,
Like the train bands, and every man engage
For a sufficient fool, to serve the stage.
And when, with much ado, you get him there,
Where he in all his glory should appear,
Your poets make him such rare things to say,
That he's more wit than any man i' th' play:
But of so ill a mingle with the rest,
As when a parrot's taught to break a jest.
Thus, aiming to be fine, they make a show,
As tawdry squires in country churches do.
Things well considered, 'tis so hard to make
A comedy, which should the knowing take,
That our dull poet, in despair to please,
Does humbly beg, by me, his writ of ease.
'Tis a land-tax, which he's too poor to pay;
You therefore must some other impost lay.
Would you but change, for serious plot and verse,
This motely garniture of fool and farce,
Nor scorn a mode, because 'tis taught at home,
Which does, like vests, our gravity become,
Our poet yields you should this play refuse:
As tradesmen, by the change of fashions, lose,
With some content, their fripperies of France,
In hope it may their staple trade advance.

John Dryden – A Short Biography

John Dryden was born on August 9th, 1631 in the village rectory of Aldwincle near Thrapston in Northamptonshire, where his maternal grandfather was Rector of All Saints Church.

Dryden was the eldest of fourteen children born to Erasmus Dryden and wife Mary Pickering, paternal grandson of Sir Erasmus Dryden, 1st Baronet (1553–1632) and wife Frances Wilkes, Puritan landowning gentry who supported the Puritan cause and Parliament.

As a boy Dryden lived in the nearby village of Titchmarsh, Northamptonshire where it is probable that he received his first education.

In 1644 he was sent to Westminster School as a King's Scholar where his headmaster was Dr. Richard Busby, a charismatic teacher but severe disciplinarian. Having recently been re-founded by Elizabeth I, Westminster now embraced a very different religious and political spirit encouraging royalism and high Anglicanism but as a humanist public school, it maintained a curriculum which trained pupils in the art of rhetoric and the presentation of arguments for both sides of a given issue. This skill would remain with Dryden and influence his later writing and thinking, as much of it displays these dialectical patterns.

His first published poem, whilst still at Westminster, was an elegy with a strong royalist flavour on the death of his schoolmate Henry, Lord Hastings from smallpox, and alludes to the execution of King Charles I, which took place on January 30th, 1649.

In 1650 Dryden was ready for University and travelled to Trinity College, Cambridge. Dryden's undergraduate years would almost certainly have followed the standard curriculum of classics, rhetoric, and mathematics.

Dryden obtained his BA in 1654, graduating top of the list for Trinity that year.

However family tragedy struck in June of the same year when Dryden's father died, leaving him some land which generated a small income, but not enough to live on.

Returning to London during The Protectorate, Dryden now obtained work with Cromwell's Secretary of State, John Thurloe. This may have been the result of influence exercised on his behalf by his cousin the Lord Chamberlain, Sir Gilbert Pickering.

At Cromwell's funeral on 23 November 1658 Dryden was in the company of the Puritan poets John Milton and Andrew Marvell. The setting was to be a sea change in English history. From Republic to Monarchy and from one set of lauded poets to what would soon become the Age of Dryden.

The start began later that year when Dryden published the first of his great poems, Heroic Stanzas (1658), a eulogy on Cromwell's death which is necessarily cautious and prudent in its emotional display.

With the Restoration of the Monarchy in 1660 Dryden celebrated in verse with Astraea Redux, an authentic royalist panegyric. In this work the interregnum is illustrated as a time of anarchy, and Charles is seen as the restorer of peace and order.

With the king now established Dryden moved quickly to place himself as the leading poet and critic of his day and transferred his allegiances to the new government.

Along with Astraea Redux, Dryden welcomed the new regime with two more panegyrics: To His Sacred Majesty: A Panegyric on his Coronation (1662) and To My Lord Chancellor (1662).

These panegyrics are occasional and written to celebrate events. Thus they are written for the nation rather than the self, but these and others put him in good standing for his eventual appointment as Poet Laureate, where a number of event poems would be required each year and speaking for the Nation and to the Nation would be the first order of duty.

These poems suggest that Dryden was looking to court a possible patron which would have given him an income and time to explore his creative ideas but no, his path instead would be to make a living in writing for publishers, not for the aristocracy, and thus ultimately for the reading public.

In November 1662 Dryden was proposed for membership in the Royal Society, and he was elected an early fellow. However, his inactivity and non payment of dues led to his expulsion in 1666.

On December 1st, 1663 Dryden married the Royalist sister of Sir Robert Howard—Lady Elizabeth Howard (died 1714). The marriage was at St. Swithin's, London, and the consent of the parents is noted on the license, though Lady Elizabeth was then about twenty-five. She was the object of some scandals, well or ill founded; it was said that Dryden had been bullied into the marriage by her brothers. A small estate in Wiltshire was settled upon them by her father. The lady's intellect and temper were apparently not good; her husband was treated as an inferior by those of her social status.

Dryden's works occasionally contain outbursts against the married state but also celebrations of the same. Little else is known of the intimate side of his marriage.

Both Dryden and his wife were warmly attached to their children. They had three sons: Charles (1666–1704), John (1668–1701), and Erasmus Henry (1669–1710). Lady Elizabeth Dryden survived her husband, but went insane soon after his death and died in 1714.

With the re-opening of the theatres after the Puritan ban, Dryden began to also write plays. His first play, The Wild Gallant, appeared in 1663 but was not successful. From 1668 on he was contracted to produce three plays a year for the King's Company, in which he became a shareholder. During the 1660s and '70s, theatrical writing was his main source of income. He led the way in Restoration comedy, his best-known works being Marriage à la Mode (1672), as well as heroic tragedy and regular tragedy, in which his greatest success was All for Love (1678). Dryden was never fully satisfied with his theatrical writings and frequently suggested that his talents were wasted on unworthy audiences.

Certainly therefore fame as a poet looked more rewarding. In 1667, around the same time his dramatic career began, he published Annus Mirabilis, a lengthy historical poem which described the English defeat of the Dutch naval fleet and the Great Fire of London in 1666. It was a modern epic in pentameter quatrains that established him as the pre-eminent poet of his generation, and was crucial in his attaining the posts of Poet Laureate (1668) and then historiographer royal (1670).

When the Great Plague of London closed the theatres in 1665 Dryden retreated to Wiltshire where he wrote Of Dramatick Poesie (1668), arguably the best of his unsystematic prefaces and essays. Dryden constantly defended his own literary practice, and Of Dramatick Poesie, the longest of his critical works, takes the form of a dialogue in which four characters—each based on a prominent contemporary, with Dryden himself as 'Neander'—debate the merits of classical, French and English drama.

He felt strongly about the relation of the poet to tradition and the creative process, and his heroic play Aureng-zebe (1675) has a prologue which denounces the use of rhyme in serious drama. His play All for Love (1678) was written in blank verse, and was to immediately follow Aureng-Zebe.

On December 18th, 1679 he was attacked in Rose Alley near his home in Covent Garden by thugs hired by fellow poet, John Wilmot, 2nd Earl of Rochester, with whom he had a long-standing conflict. Wilmot was constantly in and out of favour with the King and his own poetry was often bawdy, lewd, even obscene and made fun of the King who would often exile him from Court.

Dryden's greatest achievements were in satiric verse: the mock-heroic Mac Flecknoe, a more personal product of his Laureate years, was a lampoon circulated in manuscript and an attack on the playwright Thomas Shadwell. Dryden's main goal in the work is to "satirize Shadwell, ostensibly for his offenses against literature but more immediately we may suppose for his habitual badgering of him on the stage and in print." It is not a belittling form of satire, but rather one which makes his object great in ways which are unexpected, transferring the ridiculous into poetry. This line of satire continued with Absalom and Achitophel (1681) and The Medal (1682). Other major works from this period are the religious poems Religio Laici (1682), written from the position of a member of the Church of England; his 1683 edition of Plutarch's Lives, translated From the Greek by Several Hands in which he introduced the word biography to English readers; and The Hind and the Panther, (1687) which celebrates his conversion to Roman Catholicism.

He wrote Britannia Rediviva celebrating the birth of a son and heir to the Catholic King and Queen on June 10th, 1688. When later in the same year James II was deposed in the Glorious Revolution, Dryden's refusal to take the oaths of allegiance to the new monarchs, William and Mary, which left him out of favour at court and he had to leave his post as Poet Laureate. Thomas Shadwell, his despised rival, succeeded him. Dryden, England's greatest literary figure, was now forced to give up his public offices and live by the proceeds of his pen alone.

Dryden was an excellent translator with his own style which brought the ire of many critics. Many felt he would embellish or expand anything he felt short or curt. Dryden did not feel such expansion was a fault, arguing that as Latin is a naturally concise language it cannot be duly represented by a comparable number of words in the much larger English vocabulary. He continued with his task of translating works by Horace, Juvenal, Ovid, Lucretius, and Theocritus, a task which he found far more satisfying than writing for the stage.

In 1694 he began work on what would be his most ambitious and defining work as translator, The Works of Virgil (1697), which was published by subscription. The publication of the translation of Virgil was a national event and brought Dryden the sum of £1,400.

His final translations appeared in the volume Fables Ancient and Modern (1700), a series of episodes from Homer, Ovid, and Boccaccio, as well as modernised adaptations from Geoffrey Chaucer interspersed with Dryden's own poems. As a translator, he made great literary works in the older languages available to readers of English.

John Dryden died on May 12th, 1700, and was initially buried in St. Anne's cemetery in Soho, before being exhumed and reburied in Westminster Abbey ten days later. He was the subject of poetic eulogies, such as Luctus Brittannici: or the Tears of the British Muses; for the Death of John Dryden, Esq. (London, 1700), and The Nine Muses.

He is seen as dominating the literary life of Restoration England to such a point that the period came to be known in literary circles as the Age of Dryden. Walter Scott called him "Glorious John."

Dryden was the dominant literary figure and influence of his age. He established the heroic couplet as a standard form of English poetry by writing successful satires, religious pieces, fables, epigrams, compliments, prologues, and plays with it; he also introduced the alexandrine and triplet into the form. In his poems, translations, and criticism, he established a poetic diction appropriate to the heroic couplet—Auden referred to him as "the master of the middle style"—that was a model for his contemporaries and for much of the 18th century. The considerable loss felt by the English literary community at his death was evident in the elegies written about him. Dryden's heroic couplet went on to become the dominant poetic form of the 18th century.

What Dryden achieved in his poetry was neither the emotional excitement of the early nineteenth-century romantics nor the intellectual complexities of the metaphysicals. Although he uses formal structures such as heroic couplets, he tried to recreate the natural rhythm of speech, and he knew that different subjects need different kinds of verse. In his preface to Religio Laici he says that "the expressions of a poem designed purely for instruction ought to be plain and natural, yet majestic... The florid, elevated and figurative way is for the passions; for (these) are begotten in the soul by showing the objects out of their true proportion.... A man is to be cheated into passion, but to be reasoned into truth."

Perhaps the following illustrates Dryden and his life—"The way I have taken, is not so streight as Metaphrase, nor so loose as Paraphrase: Some things too I have omitted, and sometimes added of my own. Yet the omissions I hope, are but of Circumstances, and such as wou'd have no grace in English; and the Addition, I also hope, are easily deduc'd from Virgil's Sense. They will seem (at least I have the Vanity to think so), not struck into him, but growing out of him".

John Dryden – A Concise Bibliography

Astraea Redux, 1660
The Wild Gallant (comedy), 1663
The Indian Emperour (tragedy), 1665
Annus Mirabilis (poem), 1667
The Enchanted Island (comedy), 1667, with William D'Avenant from Shakespeare's The Tempest
Secret Love, or The Maiden Queen, 1667
An Essay of Dramatick Poesie, 1668
An Evening's Love (comedy), 1668
Tyrannick Love (tragedy), 1669
The Conquest of Granada, 1670
The Assignation, or Love in a Nunnery, 1672
Marriage à la mode, 1672
Amboyna, or the Cruelties of the Dutch to the English Merchants, 1673
The Mistaken Husband (comedy), 1674
Aureng-zebe, 1675
All for Love, 1678
Oedipus (heroic drama), 1679, an adaptation with Nathaniel Lee of Sophocles' Oedipus
Absalom and Achitophel, 1681
The Spanish Fryar, 1681
Mac Flecknoe, 1682
The Medal, 1682
Religio Laici, 1682

To the Memory of Mr. Oldham, 1684
Threnodia Augustalis, 1685
The Hind and the Panther, 1687
A Song for St. Cecilia's Day, 1687
Britannia Rediviva, 1688, written to mark the birth of a Prince of Wales.
Amphitryon, 1690
Don Sebastian (play), 1690
Creator Spirit, by whose aid, 1690. Translation of Rabanus Maurus' Veni Creator Spiritus
King Arthur, 1691
Cleomenes, 1692
The Art of Satire, 1693
Love Triumphant, 1694
The Works of Virgil, 1697
Alexander's Feast, 1697
Fables, Ancient and Modern, 1700